MONUMENT

Books by Natasha Trethewey

Poetry

DOMESTIC WORK

BELLOCQ'S OPHELIA

NATIVE GUARD

THRALL

MONUMENT

Nonfiction

BEYOND KATRINA: A MEDITATION ON
THE MISSISSIPPI GULF COAST

MONUMENT

Poems
New and Selected

NATASHA
TRETHEWEY

HOUGHTON MIFFLIN HARCOURT

BOSTON NEW YORK

hmhco.com

Library of Congress Cataloging-in-Publication Data
Names: Trethewey, Natasha D., 1966– author.
Title: Monument : poems : new and selected / Natasha Trethewey.
Description: Boston : Houghton Mifflin Harcourt, 2018.
Identifiers: LCCN 2018012255 (print) | LCCN 2018016439 (ebook) |
ISBN 9781328508690 (ebook) | ISBN 9781328507846 (hardcover)
Classification: LCC PS3570.R433 (ebook) | LCC PS3570.R433 A6 2018 (print) |
DDC 811/.54 — dc23
LC record available at https://lccn.loc.gov/2018012255

Book design by Mark R. Robinson

Printed in the United States of America
DOC 10 9 8 7 6 5 4 3
4500746058

"Invocation, 1926" by Natasha Trethewey, and "Congregation" and "Liturgy" from *Beyond Katrina* by Natasha Trethewey, copyright © 2010 by Natasha Trethewey, reprinted by permission of University of Georgia Press.

"Bellocq's Ophelia," "Letter Home," "Countess P—'s Advice for New Girls," and "Storyville Diary" copyright © 2002 by Natasha Trethewey. Reprinted from *Bellocq's Ophelia* with the permission of Graywolf Press, Minneapolis, Minnesota, www.graywolfpress.org.

"Limen," "Early Evening, Frankfort, Kentucky," "Family Portrait," "Flounder," "White Lies," "Gathering," "Picture Gallery," "Domestic Work, 1937," "Speculation, 1939," "Secular," "Signs, Oakvale, Mississippi, 1941," "Expectant," "Tableau," "At the Station," "Naola Beauty Academy, New Orleans, 1945," "Drapery Factory, Gulfport, Mississippi, 1956," "His Hands," "Self-Employment, 1970," and "Gesture of a Woman-in-Process" copyright © 2000 by Natasha Trethewey. Reprinted from *Domestic Work* with the permission of Graywolf Press, Minneapolis, Minnesota, www.graywolfpress.org.

Excerpt from "Meditation on Form and Measure" from *Black Zodiac* by Charles Wright. Copyright © 1997 by Charles Wright. Reprinted by permission of Farrar, Straus and Giroux.

For my parents—

Gwen and Rick

and

for Brett

Where no monuments exist to heroes but in the common words and deeds . . .

—from "The Great City," Walt Whitman

CONTENTS

II

from BELLOCQ'S OPHELIA

III

NATIVE GUARD

I

I V

from C O N G R E G A T I O N

V

from **T H R A L L**

V I

A R T I C U L A T I O N

Imperatives for Carrying On
in the Aftermath

Do not hang your head or clench your fists
when even your friend, after hearing the story,
says, *My mother would never put up with that.*

Fight the urge to rattle off statistics: that,
more often, a woman who chooses to leave
is then murdered. The hundredth time

your father says, *But she hated violence,*
why would she marry a guy like that?—
don't waste your breath explaining, again,

how abusers wait, are patient, that they
don't beat you on the first date, sometimes
not even the first few years of a marriage.

Keep an impassive face whenever you hear
Stand By Your Man, and let go your rage
when you recall those words were advice

given your mother. Try to forget the first
trial, before she was dead, when the charge
was only *attempted murder;* don't belabor

the thinking or the sentence that allowed
her ex-husband's release a year later, or
the juror who said, *It's a domestic issue*—

they should work it out themselves. Just
breathe when, after you read your poems
about grief, a woman asks, *Do you think*

your mother was weak for men? Learn
to ignore subtext. Imagine a thought-
cloud above your head, dark and heavy

with the words you cannot say; let silence
rain down. Remember you were told,
by your famous professor, that you should

write about something else, *unburden*
yourself of the death of your mother and
just pour your heart out in the poems.

Ask yourself what's in your heart, that
reliquary—blood locket and seedbed—and
contend with what it means, the folk saying

you learned from a Korean poet in Seoul:
that *one does not bury the mother's body*
in the ground but in the chest, or—like you—

you carry her corpse on your back.

I

from

DOMESTIC WORK

Limen

All day I've listened to the industry
of a single woodpecker, worrying the catalpa tree
just outside my window. Hard at his task,

his body is a hinge, a door knocker
to the cluttered house of memory in which
I can almost see my mother's face.

She is there, again, beyond the tree,
its slender pods and heart-shaped leaves,
hanging wet sheets on the line — each one

a thin white screen between us. So insistent
is this woodpecker, I'm sure he must be
looking for something else — not simply

the beetles and grubs inside, but some other gift
the tree might hold. All day he's been at work,
tireless, making the green hearts flutter.

Early Evening, Frankfort, Kentucky

It is 1965. I am not yet born, only
a fullness beneath the Empire waist
of my mother's blue dress.

The ruffles at her neck are waves
of light in my father's eyes. He carries
a slim volume, leather-bound, poems

to read as they walk. The long road
past the college, through town,
rises and falls before them,

the blue hills shimmering at twilight.
The stacks at the distillery exhale,
and my parents breathe evening air

heady and sweet as Kentucky bourbon.
They are young and full of laughter,
the sounds in my mother's throat

rippling down into my blood.
My mother, who will not reach
forty-one, steps into the middle

of a field, lies down among clover
and sweet grass, right here, right now —
dead center of her life.

Family Portrait

Before the picture man comes
Mama and I spend the morning
cleaning the family room. She hums
Motown, doles out chores, a warning —

He has no legs, she says. *Don't stare.*
I'm first to the door when he rings.
My father and uncle lift his chair
onto the porch, arrange his things

near the place his feet would be.
He poses our only portrait — my father
sitting, Mama beside him, and me
in between. I watch him bother

the space for knees, shins, scratching air
as — years later — I'd itch for what's not there.

Flounder

Here, she said, *put this on your head.*
She handed me a hat.
You 'bout as white as your dad,
and you gone stay like that.

Aunt Sugar rolled her nylons down
around each bony ankle,
and I rolled down my white knee socks
letting my thin legs dangle,

circling them just above water
and silver backs of minnows
flitting here then there between
the sunspots and the shadows.

This is how you hold the pole
to cast the line out straight.
Now put that worm on your hook,
throw it out, and wait.

She sat spitting tobacco juice
into a coffee cup.
Hunkered down when she felt the bite,
jerked the pole straight up

reeling and tugging hard at the fish
that wriggled and tried to fight back.
A flounder, she said, *and you can tell*
'cause one of its sides is black.

The other side is white, she said.
It landed with a thump.
I stood there watching that fish flip-flop,
switch sides with every jump.

White Lies

The lies I could tell,
when I was growing up
light-bright, near-white,
high-yellow, red-boned
in a black place,
were just white lies.

I could easily tell the white folks
that we lived uptown,
not in that pink and green
shanty-fied shotgun section
along the tracks. I could act
like my homemade dresses
came straight out the window
of Maison Blanche. I could even
keep quiet, quiet as kept,
like the time a white girl said
(squeezing my hand), *Now*
we have three of us in this class.

But I paid for it every time
Mama found out.
She laid her hands on me,
then washed out my mouth
with Ivory soap. *This
is to purify,* she said,
and cleanse your lying tongue.
Believing her, I swallowed suds
thinking they'd work
from the inside out.

Gathering

FOR SUGAR

Through tall grass, heavy
from rain, my aunt and I wade
into cool fruit trees.

Near us, dragonflies
light on the clothesline, each touch
rippling to the next.

Green-black beetles swarm
the fruit, wings droning motion,
wet figs glistening.

We sigh, click our tongues,
our fingers reaching in, then
plucking what is left.

Underripe figs, green,
hard as jewels — these we save,
hold in deep white bowls.

She puts them to light
on the windowsill, tells me
to *wait, learn patience*.

I touch them each day,
watch them turn gold, grow sweet,
and give sweetness back.

I begin to see
our lives are like this — we take
what we need of light.

We glisten, preserve
handpicked days in memory,
our minds' dark pantry.

Picture Gallery

In a tight corner of the house, we'd kept
the light-up portraits of Kennedy and King,
side by side, long after the bulbs burned out —

cords tangling on the floor, and the patina
of rust slowly taking the filigreed frames.

Then, my grandmother wanted more *Art* —
something beautiful to look at, she said.
At the fabric store she bought bolts of cloth

printed with natural scenes — far-off views
of mountains, owls on snowy boughs.

I donated the scenic backdrop that came
with a model horse — a yellowed vista
of wheat fields, a wagon, and one long road.

Back home, we gathered pinecones
and branches, staples and glue, then hung

the fabric, big as windows, in the dark
hallway. The fresh boughs we stapled on
stuck out in relief. We breathed green air,

and the owls — instead — peered in at us,
our lives suddenly beautiful, then.

Domestic Work

FOR LERETTA DIXON TURNBOUGH (LEE)

JUNE 22, 1916–JULY 28, 2008

I shirk not. I long for work. I pant for a life full of striving.

—W.E.B. Du Bois

1. DOMESTIC WORK, 1937

All week she's cleaned
someone else's house,
stared down her own face
in the shine of copper-
bottomed pots, polished
wood, toilets she'd pull
the lid to—that look saying

Let's make a change, girl.

But Sunday mornings are hers—
church clothes starched
and hanging, a record spinning
on the console, the whole house
dancing. She raises the shades,
washes the rooms in light,
buckets of water, Octagon soap.

Cleanliness is next to godliness . . .

Windows and doors flung wide,
curtains two-stepping
forward and back, neck bones
bumping in the pot, a choir
of clothes clapping on the line.

Nearer my God to Thee . . .

She beats time on the rugs,
blows dust from the broom
like dandelion spores, each one
a wish for something better.

2. SPECULATION, 1939

First, the moles on each hand —
That's money by the pan —

and always the New Year's cabbage
and black-eyed peas. Now this,
another remembered adage,
her palms itching with promise,

she swears by the signs — *Money coming soon.*
But from where? Her left-eye twitch
says she'll see the boon.
Good — she's tired of the elevator switch,

those closed-in spaces, white men's
sideways stares. Nothing but
time to think, make plans
each time the doors slide shut.

What's to be gained from this New Deal?
Something finer like beauty school
or a milliner's shop — she loves the feel
of marcelled hair, felt and tulle,

not this all-day standing around,
not that elevator lurching up, then down.

3. SECULAR

Workweek's end
and there's enough
block-ice in the box
to chill a washtub of colas
and one large melon,
dripping green.
After service, each house opens
heavy doors to street and woods,
one clear shot from front to back —
bullet, breeze, or holler.
A neighbor's *Yoo-hoo* reaches her
out back, lolling, pulling in wash,
pillow slips billowing
around her head like clouds.
Up the block,
a brand-new Grafonola,
parlor music, blues parlando —
Big Mama, Ma Rainey, Bessie —
baby shake that thing like a saltshaker.
Lipstick, nylons
and she's out the door,
tipping past the church house,
Dixie Peach in her hair,
greased forehead shining
like gospel, like gold.

4. SIGNS, OAKVALE, MISSISSIPPI, 1941

The first time she leaves home is with a man.
On Highway 49, heading north, she watches
the pine woods roll by, and counts on one hand
dead possum along the road, crows in splotches
of light — she knows to watch the signs for luck.
He has a fine car, she thinks. *And money green
enough to buy a dream* — more than she could tuck
under the mattress, in a Bible, or fold between
her powdered breasts. He'd promised land to farm
back home, new dresses, a house where she'd be
queen. (*Was that gap in his teeth cause for alarm?*)
The cards said *go.* She could roam the Delta, see
things she'd never seen. Outside her window,
nothing but cotton and road signs — *stop* or *slow.*

5. EXPECTANT

Nights are hardest, the swelling,
tight and low (a girl), Delta heat,

and that woodsy silence a zephyred hush.
So how to keep busy? Wind the clocks,

measure out time to check the window,
or listen hard for his car on the road.

Small tasks done and undone, a floor
swept clean. She can fill a room

with a loud clear alto, broom-dance
right out the back door, her heavy footsteps

a parade beneath the stars. Honeysuckle
fragrant as perfume, nightlife

a steady insect hum. Still, she longs
for the Quarter — lights, riverboats churning,

the tinkle of ice in a slim bar glass.
Each night a refrain, its plain blue notes

carrying her, slightly swaying, home.

6. TABLEAU

At breakfast, the scent of lemons,
just picked, yellowing on the sill.
At the table, the man and woman.

Between them, a still life:
shallow bowl, damask plums
in one square of morning light.

The woman sips tea
from a chipped blue cup, turning it,
avoiding the rough white edge.

The man, his thumb pushing deep
toward the pit, peels taut skin
clean from plum flesh.

The woman watches his hands,
the pale fruit darkening
wherever he's pushed too hard.

She is thinking *seed,* the hardness
she'll roll on her tongue,
a beginning. One by one,

the man fills the bowl with globes
that glisten. *Translucent,* he thinks.
The woman, now, her cup tilting

empty, sees, for the first time,
the hairline crack
that has begun to split the bowl in half.

7. AT THE STATION

The blue light was my blues,
and the red light was my mind.

— *Robert Johnson*

The man, turning, moves away
from the platform. Growing smaller,
he does not say

Come back. She won't. Each
glowing light dims
the farther it moves from reach,

the train pulling clean
out of the station. The woman sits
facing where she's been.

She's chosen her place with care —
each window another eye, another
way of seeing what's back there:

heavy blossoms in afternoon rain
spilling scent and glistening sex.
Everything dripping green.

Blue shade, leaves swollen like desire.
A man motioning *nothing.*
No words. His mind on fire.

8. NAOLA BEAUTY ACADEMY,
NEW ORLEANS, 1945

Made hair? The girls here
put a press on your head
last two weeks. No naps.

They learning. See the basins?
This where we wash. Yeah,
it's hot. July jam.

Stove always on. Keep the combs
hot. Lee and Ida bumping hair
right now. Best two.

Ida got a natural touch.
Don't burn nobody.
Her own's a righteous mass.

Lee, now she used to sew.
Her fingers steady
from them tiny needles.

She can fix some bad hair.
Look how she lay them waves.
Light, slight, and polite.

Not a one out of place.

9. DRAPERY FACTORY,
GULFPORT, MISSISSIPPI, 1956

She made the trip daily, though
later she would not remember
how far to tell the grandchildren—
Better that way.
She could keep those miles
a secret, and her black face
and black hands, and the pink bottoms
of her black feet
a minor inconvenience.

She does remember the men
she worked for, and that often
she sat side by side
with white women, all of them
bent over, pushing into the hum
of the machines, their right calves
tensed against the pedals.

Her lips tighten speaking
of quitting time when
the colored women filed out slowly
to have their purses checked,
the insides laid open and exposed
by the boss's hand.

But then she laughs
when she recalls the soiled Kotex
she saved, stuffed into a bag
in her purse, and Adam's look
on one white man's face, his hand
deep in knowledge.

10. HIS HANDS

His hands will never be large enough.
Not for the woman who sees in his face
the father she can't remember,
or her first husband, the soldier with two wives—
all the men who would only take.
Not large enough to deflect
the sharp edges of her words.

Still he tries to prove himself in work,
his callused hands heaving crates
all day on the docks, his pay twice spent.
He brings home what he can, buckets of crabs
from his morning traps, a few green bananas.

His supper waits in the warming oven,
the kitchen dark, the screens hooked.
He thinks *Make the hands gentle*
as he raps lightly on the back door.
He has never had a key.

Putting her hands to his, she pulls him in,
sets him by the stove. Slowly, she rubs oil
into his cracked palms, drawing out soreness
from the swells, removing splinters, taking
whatever his hands will give.

Who to be today? So many choices,
all that natural human hair piled high,
curled and flipped — style after style
perched, each on its Styrofoam head.
Maybe an upsweep, or finger waves
with a ponytail. Not a day passes
that she goes unkempt —
Never know who might stop by —
now that she works at home
pacing the cutting table,
or pumping the stiff pedal
of the bought-on-time Singer.

Most days, she dresses for the weather,
relentless sun, white heat. The one tree
nearest her workroom, a mimosa,
its whimsy of pink puffs cut back
for a child's swing set. And now, grandchildren —
it's come to this — a frenzy of shouts,
the constant *slap* of an old screen door.
At least the radio still swings jazz
just above the noise, and

ah yes, the window unit—leaky at best.
Sometimes she just stands still, lets
ice water drip onto upturned wrists.
Up under that wig, her head
sweating, hot as an idea.

Gesture of a Woman in Process

FROM A PHOTOGRAPH BY
CLIFTON JOHNSON, 1902

In the foreground, two women,
their squinting faces
creased into texture—

a deep relief—the lines
like palms of hands
I could read if I could touch.

Around them, their dailiness:
clotheslines sagged with linens,
a patch of greens and yams,

buckets of peas for shelling.
One woman pauses for the picture.
The other won't be still.

Even now, her hands circling,
the white blur of her apron
still in motion.

II

from

BELLOCQ'S OPHELIA

Nevertheless, the camera's rendering of reality must always hide more than it discloses.

—Susan Sontag

Bellocq's Ophelia

FROM A PHOTOGRAPH, CIRCA 1912

In Millais's painting, Ophelia dies faceup,
eyes and mouth open as if caught in the gasp
of her last word or breath, flowers and reeds
growing out of the pond, floating on the surface
around her. The young woman who posed
lay in a bath for hours, shivering,
catching cold, perhaps imagining fish
tangling in her hair or nibbling a dark mole
raised upon her white skin. Ophelia's final gaze
aims skyward, her palms curling open
as if she's just said, *Take me.*

I think of her when I see Bellocq's photograph—
a woman posed on a wicker divan, her hair
spilling over. Around her, flowers—
on a pillow, on a thick carpet. Even
the ravages of this old photograph
bloom like water lilies across her thigh.
How long did she hold there, this other
Ophelia, nameless inmate of Storyville,
naked, her nipples offered up hard with cold?

The small mound of her belly, the pale hair
of her pubis — these things — her body
there for the taking. But in her face, a dare.
Staring into the camera, she seems to pull
all movement from her slender limbs
and hold it in her heavy-lidded eyes.
Her body limp as dead Ophelia's,
her lips poised to open, to speak.

Letter Home

Four weeks have passed since I left, and still
I must write to you of no work. I've worn down
the soles and walked through the tightness
of my new shoes, calling upon the merchants,
their offices bustling. All the while I kept thinking
my plain English and good writing would secure
for me some modest position. Though I dress each day
in my best, hands covered with the lace gloves
you crocheted—no one needs a *girl*. How flat
the word sounds, and heavy. My purse thins.
I spend foolishly to make an appearance of quiet
industry, to mask the desperation that tightens
my throat. I sit watching—

though I pretend not to notice—the dark maids
ambling by with their white charges. Do I deceive
anyone? Were they to see my hands, brown
as your dear face, they'd know I'm not quite
what I pretend to be. I walk these streets
a white woman, or so I think, until I catch the eyes
of some stranger upon me, and I must lower mine,
a *negress* again. There are enough things here
to remind me who I am. Mules lumbering through
the crowded streets send me into reverie, their footfall
the sound of a pointer and chalk hitting the blackboard
at school, only louder. Then there are women, clicking

their tongues in conversation, carrying their loads
on their heads. Their husky voices, the washpots
and irons of the laundresses call to me. Here,

I thought not to do the work I once did, back-bending
and domestic; my schooling a gift — even those half days
at picking time, listening to Miss J —. How
I'd come to know words, the recitations I practiced
to sound like her, lilting, my sentences curling up
or trailing off at the ends. I read my books until
I nearly broke their spines, and in the cotton field,
I repeated whole sections I'd learned by heart,
spelling each word in my head to make a picture
I could see, as well as a weight I could feel
in my mouth. So now, even as I write this
and think of you at home, *Goodbye*

is the waving map of your palm, is
a stone on my tongue.

Countess P —'s Advice for New Girls

STORYVILLE, 1910

Look, this is a high-class house—polished
mahogany, potted ferns, rugs two inches thick.
The mirrored parlor multiplies everything—

one glass of champagne is twenty. You'll see
yourself a hundred times. For our customers
you must learn to be watched. Empty

your thoughts—think, if you do, only
of your swelling purse. Hold still as if
you sit for a painting. Catch light

in the hollow of your throat; let shadow dwell
in your navel and beneath the curve
of your breasts. See yourself through his eyes—

your neck stretched long and slender, your back
arched—the awkward poses he might capture
in stone. Let his gaze animate you, then move

as it flatters you most. Wait to be
asked to speak. Think of yourself as molten glass—
expand and quiver beneath the weight of his breath.

Don't pretend you don't know what I mean.
Become what you must. Let him see whatever
he needs. Train yourself not to look back.

Storyville Diary

1. NAMING

I cannot now remember the first word
I learned to write — perhaps it was my name,
Ophelia, in tentative strokes, a banner
slanting across my tablet at school, or inside
the cover of some treasured book. Leaving
my home today, I feel even more the need
for some new words to mark this journey,
like the naming of a child — *Queen, Lovely,*
Hope — marking even the humblest beginnings
in the shanties. My own name was a chant
over the washboard, a song to guide me
into sleep. Once, my mother pushed me toward
a white man in our front room. *Your father,*
she whispered. *He's the one that named you, girl.*

2. FATHER

There is but little I recall of him — how
I feared his visits, though he would bring gifts:
apples, candy, a toothbrush and powder.
In exchange, I must present fingernails
and ears, open my mouth to show the teeth.
Then I'd recite my lessons, my voice low.
I would stumble over a simple word, say
lay for *lie,* and he would stop me there. How
I wanted him to like me, think me smart,
a delicate colored girl — not the wild
pickaninny roaming the fields, barefoot.
I search now for his face among the men
I pass in the streets, fear the day a man
enters my room both customer and father.

3. BELLOCQ

APRIL 1911

There comes a quiet man now to my room—
Papá Bellocq, his camera on his back.
He wants *nothing,* he says, but to take me
as I would arrange myself, fully clothed—
a brooch at my throat, my white hat angled
just so—*or not,* the smooth map of my flesh
awash in afternoon light. In my room
everything's a prop for his composition—
brass spittoon in the corner, the silver
mirror, brush and comb of my toilette.
I try to pose as I think he would like—shy
at first, then bolder. I'm not so foolish
that I don't know this photograph *we* make
will bear the stamp of his name, not mine.

4. BLUE BOOK

JUNE 1911

I wear my best gown for the picture —
white silk with seed pearls and ostrich feathers —
my hair in a loose chignon. Behind me,
Bellocq's black scrim just covers the laundry —
tea towels, bleached and frayed, drying on the line.
I look away from his lens to appear
demure, to attract those guests not wanting
the lewd sights of Emma Johnson's circus.
Countess writes my description for the book —
"Violet," a fair-skinned beauty, recites
poetry and soliloquies; nightly
she performs her tableau vivant, becomes
a living statue, an object of art —
and I fade again into someone I'm not.

5. PORTRAIT #1

Here, I am to look casual, even
frowsy, though still queen of my boudoir.
A moment caught as if by accident—
pictures crooked on the walls, newspaper
sprawled on the dresser, a bit of pale silk
spilling from a drawer, and my slip pulled
below my white shoulders, décolleté,
black stockings, legs crossed easy as a man's.
All of it contrived except for the way
the flowered walls dominate the backdrop
and close in on me as I pose, my hand
at rest on my knee, a single finger
raised, arching toward the camera—a gesture
before speech, before the first word comes out.

6. PORTRAIT #2

I pose nude for this photograph, awkward,
one arm folded behind my back, the other
limp at my side. Seated, I raise my chin,
my back so straight I imagine the bones
separating in my spine, my neck lengthening
like evening shadow. When I see this plate
I try to recall what I was thinking—
how not to be exposed, though naked, how
to wear skin like a garment, seamless.
Bellocq thinks I'm right for the camera, keeps
coming to my room. *These plates are fragile,*
he says, showing me how easy it is
to shatter this image of myself, how
a quick scratch carves a scar across my chest.

7. PHOTOGRAPHY

OCTOBER 1911

Bellocq talks to me about light, shows me
how to use shadow, how to fill the frame
with objects — their intricate positions.
I thrill to the magic of it — silver
crystals like constellations of stars
arranging on film. In the negative
the whole world reverses, my black dress turned
white, my skin blackened to pitch. *Inside out,*
I said, thinking of what I've tried to hide.
I follow him now, watch him take pictures.
I look at what he can see through his lens
and what he cannot — silverfish behind
the walls, the yellow tint of a faded bruise —
other things here, what the camera misses.

8. DISCLOSURE

JANUARY 1912

When Bellocq doesn't like a photograph
he scratches across the plate. But I know
other ways to obscure a face — paint it
with rouge and powder, shades lighter than skin,
don a black velvet mask. I've learned to keep
my face behind the camera, my lens aimed
at a dream of my own making. What power
I find in transforming what is real — a room
flushed with light, calculated disarray.
Today I tried to capture a redbird
perched on the tall hedge. As my shutter fell,
he lifted in flight, a vivid blur above
the clutter just beyond the hedge — garbage,
rats licking the insides of broken eggs.

9. SPECTRUM

No sun, and the city's a dull palette
of gray—weathered ships docked at the quay, rats
dozing in the hull, drizzle slicking dark stones
of the streets. Mornings such as these, I walk
among the weary, their eyes sunken
as if each body, diseased and dying,
would pull itself inside, back to the shining
center. In the cemetery, all the rest,
their resolute bones stacked against the pull
of the Gulf. Here, another world teems—flies
buzzing the meat-stand, cockroaches crisscrossing
the banquette, the curve and flex of larvae
in the cisterns, and mosquitoes skimming
flat water like skaters on a frozen pond.

10. (SELF) PORTRAIT

MARCH 1912

On the crowded street I want to stop
time, hold it captive in my dark chamber —
a train's sluggish pull out of the station,
passengers waving through open windows,
the dull faces of those left on the platform.
Once, I boarded a train; leaving my home,
I watched the red sky, the low sun glowing —
an ember I could blow into flame — night
falling and my past darkening behind me.
Now I wait for a departure, the whistle's
shrill calling. The first time I tried this shot
I thought of my mother shrinking against
the horizon — so distracted, I looked into
a capped lens, saw only my own clear eye.

III

NATIVE GUARD

For my mother
Gwendolyn Ann Turnbough
in memory

Memory is a cemetery
I've visited once or twice, white
                    ubiquitous and the set-aside

Everywhere under foot . . .

                              —Charles Wright

Theories of Time and Space

You can get there from here, though
there's no going home.

Everywhere you go will be somewhere
you've never been. Try this:

head south on Mississippi 49, one-
by-one mile markers ticking off

another minute of your life. Follow this
to its natural conclusion — dead end

at the coast, the pier at Gulfport where
riggings of shrimp boats are loose stitches

in a sky threatening rain. Cross over
the man-made beach, 26 miles of sand

dumped on the mangrove swamp — buried
terrain of the past. Bring only

what you must carry — tome of memory,
its random blank pages. On the dock

where you board the boat for Ship Island,
someone will take your picture:

the photograph — who you were —
will be waiting when you return.

I

I'm going there to meet my mother
She said she'd meet me when I come
I'm only going over Jordan
I'm only going over home.

—Traditional

The Southern Crescent

1

In 1959 my mother is boarding a train.
She is barely sixteen, her one large grip
bulging with homemade dresses, whisper
of crinoline and lace, her name stitched
inside each one. She is leaving behind
the dirt roads of Mississippi, the film
of red dust around her ankles, the thin
whistle of wind through the floorboards
of the shotgun house, the very idea of home.

Ahead of her, days of travel, one town
after the next, and *California* — a word
she can't stop repeating. Over and over
she will practice meeting her father, imagine
how he must look, how different now
from the one photo she has of him. She will
look at it once more, pulling into the station
at Los Angeles, and then again and again
on the platform, no one like him in sight.

2

The year the old Crescent makes its last run,
my mother insists we ride it together.
We leave Gulfport late morning, heading east.
Years before, we rode together to meet
another man, my father, waiting for us
as our train derailed. I don't recall how
she must have held me, how her face sank
as she realized, again, the uncertainty
of it all—that trip, too, gone wrong. Today,

she is sure we can leave home, bound only
for whatever awaits us, the sun now
setting behind us, the rails humming
like anticipation, the train pulling us
toward the end of another day. I watch
each small town pass before my window
until the light goes, and the reflection
of my mother's face appears, clearer now
as evening comes on, dark and certain.

Genus Narcissus

Faire daffadills, we weep to see
You haste away so soone.

      —Robert Herrick

The road I walked home from school
was dense with trees and shadow, creek-side,
and lit by yellow daffodils, early blossoms

bright against winter's last gray days.
I must have known they grew wild, thought
no harm in taking them. So I did —

gathering up as many as I could hold,
then presenting them, in a jar, to my mother.
She put them on the sill, and I sat nearby

watching light bend through the glass,
day easing into evening, proud of myself
for giving my mother some small thing.

Childish vanity. I must have seen in them
some measure of myself — the slender stems,
each blossom a head lifted up

toward praise, or bowed to meet its reflection.
Walking home those years ago, I knew nothing
of Narcissus or the daffodils' short spring —

how they'd dry like graveside flowers, rustling
when the wind blew — a whisper, treacherous,
from the sill. *Be taken with yourself,*

they said to me; *Die early,* to my mother.

Graveyard Blues

It rained the whole time we were laying her down;
Rained from church to grave when we put her down.
The suck of mud at our feet was a hollow sound.

When the preacher called out I held up my hand;
When he called for a witness I raised my hand —
Death stops the body's work, the soul's a journeyman.

The sun came out when I turned to walk away,
Glared down on me as I turned and walked away —
My back to my mother, leaving her where she lay.

The road going home was pocked with holes,
That home-going road's always full of holes;
Though we slow down, time's wheel still rolls.

      I wander now among names of the dead:
      My mother's name, stone pillow for my head.

What the Body Can Say

Even in stone the gesture is unmistakable —
the man upright, though on his knees, spine

arched, head flung back, and, covering his eyes,
his fingers spread across his face. I think

grief, and since he's here, in the courtyard
of the divinity school, *what he might ask of God.*

How easy it is to read this body's language,
or those gestures we've come to know — the raised thumb

that is both a symbol of agreement and the request
for a ride, the two fingers held up that once meant

victory, then *peace.* But what was my mother saying
that day not long before her death — her face tilted up

at me, her mouth falling open, wordless, just as
we open our mouths in church to take in the wafer,

meaning *communion?* What matters is context —
the side of the road, or that my mother wanted

something I still can't name: what, kneeling,
my face behind my hands, I might ask of God.

Photograph: Ice Storm, 1971

Why the rough edge of beauty? Why
the tired face of a woman, suffering,
made luminous by the camera's eye?

Or the storm that drives us inside
for days, power lines down, food rotting
in the refrigerator, while outside

the landscape glistens beneath a glaze
of ice? Why remember anything
but the wonder of those few days,

the iced trees, each leaf in its glassy case?
The picture we took that first morning,
the front yard a beautiful, strange place —

why on the back has someone made a list
of our names, the date, the event: nothing
of what's inside — mother, stepfather's fist?

What Is Evidence

Not the fleeting bruises she'd cover
with makeup, a dark patch as if imprint
of a scope she'd pressed her eye too close to,
looking for a way out, nor the quiver
in the voice she'd steady, leaning
into a pot of bones on the stove. Not
the teeth she wore in place of her own, or
the official document — its seal
and smeared signature — fading already,
the edges wearing. Not the tiny marker
with its dates, her name, abstract as history.
Only the landscape of her body — splintered
clavicle, pierced temporal — her thin bones
settling a bit each day, the way all things do.

Letter

At the post office, I dash a note to a friend,
tell her I've just moved in, gotten settled, that

I'm now rushing off on an errand—except
that I write *errant,* a slip between letters,

each with an upright backbone anchoring it
to the page. One has with it the fullness

of possibility, a shape almost like the O
my friend's mouth will make when she sees

my letter in her box; the other, a mark that crosses
like the flat line of your death, the symbol

over the church house door, the ashes on your forehead
some Wednesday I barely remember.

What was I saying? I had to cross the word out,
start again, explain what I know best

because of the way you left me: how suddenly
a simple errand, a letter—everything—can go wrong.

After Your Death

First, I emptied the closets of your clothes,
threw out the bowl of fruit, bruised
from your touch, left empty the jars

you bought for preserves. The next morning,
birds rustled the fruit trees, and later
when I twisted a ripe fig loose from its stem,

I found it half eaten, the other side
already rotting, or — like another I plucked
and split open — being taken from the inside:

a swarm of insects hollowing it. I'm too late,
again, another space emptied by loss.
Tomorrow, the bowl I have yet to fill.

Myth

I was asleep while you were dying.
It's as if you slipped through some rift, a hollow
I make between my slumber and my waking,

the Erebus I keep you in, still trying
not to let go. You'll be dead again tomorrow,
but in dreams you live. So I try taking

you back into morning. Sleep-heavy, turning,
my eyes open, I find you do not follow.
Again and again, this constant forsaking.

*

Again and again, this constant forsaking:
my eyes open, I find you do not follow.
You back into morning, sleep-heavy, turning.

But in dreams you live. So I try taking,
not to let go. You'll be dead again tomorrow.
The Erebus I keep you in — still, trying —

I make between my slumber and my waking.
It's as if you slipped through some rift, a hollow.
I was asleep while you were dying.

At Dusk

At first I think she is calling a child,
my neighbor, leaning through her doorway
at dusk, streetlamps just starting to hum
the backdrop of evening. Then I hear
the high-pitched wheedling we send out
to animals who know only sound, not
the meanings of our words—*here here*—
nor how they sometimes fall short.
In another yard, beyond my neighbor's
sight, the cat lifts her ears, turns first
toward the voice, then back
to the constellation of fireflies flickering
near her head. It's as if she can't decide
whether to leap over the low hedge,
the neat row of flowers, and bound
onto the porch, into the steady circle
of light, or stay where she is: luminous
possibility—all that would keep her
away from home—flitting before her.
I listen as my neighbor's voice trails off.
She's given up calling for now, left me
to imagine her inside the house waiting,
perhaps in a chair in front of the TV,
or walking around, doing small tasks;
left me to wonder that I too might lift
my voice, sure of someone out there,
send it over the lines stitching here
to there, certain the sounds I make
are enough to call someone home.

II

Everybody knows about Mississippi.

—Nina Simone

Pilgrimage

Here, the Mississippi carved
    its mud-dark path, a graveyard

for skeletons of sunken riverboats.
    Here, the river changed its course,

turning away from the city
    as one turns, forgetting, from the past—

the abandoned bluffs, land sloping up
    above the river's bend—where now

the Yazoo fills the Mississippi's empty bed.
    Here, the dead stand up in stone, white

marble, on Confederate Avenue. I stand
    on ground once hollowed by a web of caves;

they must have seemed like catacombs,
    in 1863, to the woman sitting in her parlor,

candlelit, underground. I can see her
    listening to shells explode, writing herself

into history, asking *what is to become*
    of all the living things in this place?

This whole city is a grave. Every spring —
        Pilgrimage — the living come to mingle

with the dead, brush against their cold shoulders
        in the long hallways, listen all night

to their silence and indifference, relive
        their dying on the green battlefield.

At the museum, we marvel at their clothes —
        preserved under glass — so much smaller

than our own, as if those who wore them
        were only children. We sleep in their beds,

the old mansions hunkered on the bluffs, draped
        in flowers — funereal — a blur

of petals against the river's gray.
        The brochure in my room calls this

living history. The brass plate on the door reads
        Prissy's Room. A window frames

the river's crawl toward the Gulf. In my dream,
        the ghost of history lies down beside me,

rolls over, pins me beneath a heavy arm.

Scenes from a Documentary History of Mississippi

1. KING COTTON, 1907

From every corner of the photograph, flags wave down
the main street in Vicksburg. Stacked to form an arch,
the great bales of cotton rise up from the ground

like a giant swell, a wave of history flooding the town.
When Roosevelt arrives—a parade—the band will march,
and from every street corner, flags wave down.

Words on a banner, *Cotton, America's King,* have the sound
of progress. This is two years before the South's countermarch—
the great bolls of cotton, risen up from the ground,

infested with boll weevils—a plague, biblical, all around.
Now, negro children ride the bales, clothes stiff with starch.
From up high, in the photograph, they wave flags down

for the President who will walk through the arch, bound
for the future, his back to us. The children, on their perch—
those great bales of cotton rising up from the ground—

stare out at us. Cotton surrounds them, a swell, a great mound
bearing them up, back toward us. From the arch,
from every corner of the photograph, flags wave down,
and great bales of cotton rise up from the ground.

2. GLYPH, ABERDEEN, 1913

The child's head droops as if in sleep.
Stripped to the waist, in profile, he's balanced
on the man's lap. The man, gaunt in his overalls,
cradles the child's thin arm — the sharp elbow, white
signature of skin and bone — pulls it forward
to show the deformity — the humped back, curve
of spine — punctuating the routine hardships
of their lives: how the child must follow him
into the fields, haunting the long hours
slumped beside a sack, his body asking
how much cotton? or in the kitchen, leaning
into the icebox, *how much food?* or
kneeling beside him at the church house,
why, Lord, why? They pose as if to say
Look, this is the outline of suffering:
the child shouldering it — a mound
like dirt heaped on a grave.

3. FLOOD

They have arrived on the back
of the swollen river, the barge
dividing it, their few belongings
clustered about their feet. Above them
the National Guard hunkers
on the levee; rifles tight in their fists,
they block the path to high ground.
One group of black refugees,

the caption tells us, *was ordered*
to sing their passage onto land,
like a chorus of prayer — their tongues
the tongues of dark bells. Here,
the camera finds them still. Posed
as if for a school-day portrait,
children lace fingers in their laps.
One boy gestures allegiance, right hand
over the heart's charged beating.

The great river all around, the barge
invisible beneath their feet, they fix
on what's before them: the opening
in the sight of a rifle; the camera's lens;
the muddy cleft between barge and dry land —
all of it aperture, the captured moment's
chasm in time. Here, in the angled light
of 1927, they are refugees from history:
the barge has brought them this far;
they are waiting to disembark.

4. YOU ARE LATE

The sun is high and the child's shadow,
almost fully beneath her, touches the sole
of her bare foot on concrete. Even though
it must be hot, she takes the step; her goal

to read is the subject of this shot — a book
in her hand, the library closed, the door
just out of reach. Stepping up, she must look
at the two signs, read them slowly once more.

The first one, in pale letters, barely shows
against the white background. Though she will read
Greenwood Public Library for Negroes,
the other, bold letters on slate, will lead

her away, out of the frame, a finger
pointing left. I want to call her, say *wait.*
But this is history: she can't linger.
She'll read the sign that I read: *You Are Late.*

Native Guard

*If this war is to be forgotten, I ask in the name of all
things sacred what shall men remember?*

—Frederick Douglass

NOVEMBER 1862

Truth be told, I do not want to forget
anything of my former life: the landscape's
song of bondage—dirge in the river's throat
where it churns into the Gulf, wind in trees
choked with vines. I thought to carry with me
want of freedom though I had been freed,
remembrance not constant recollection.
Yes: I was born a slave, at harvest time,
in the Parish of Ascension; I've reached
thirty-three with history of one younger
inscribed upon my back. I now use ink
to keep record, a closed book, not the lure
of memory—flawed, changeful—that dulls the lash
for the master, sharpens it for the slave.

DECEMBER 1862

For the slave, having a master sharpens
the bend into work, the way the sergeant
moves us now to perfect battalion drill,
dress parade. Still, we're called supply units—

not infantry — and so we dig trenches,
haul burdens for the army no less heavy
than before. I heard the colonel call it
nigger work. Half rations make our work
familiar still. We take those things we need
from the Confederates' abandoned homes:
salt, sugar, even this journal, near full
with someone else's words, overlapped now,
crosshatched beneath mine. On every page,
his story intersecting with my own.

JANUARY 1863

O how history intersects — my own
berth upon a ship called the *Northern Star*
and I'm delivered into a new life,
Fort Massachusetts: a great irony —
both path and destination of freedom
I'd not dared to travel. Here, now, I walk
ankle-deep in sand, fly-bitten, nearly
smothered by heat, and yet I can look out
upon the Gulf and see the surf breaking,
tossing the ships, the great gunboats bobbing
on the water. And are we not the same,
slaves in the hands of the master, destiny?
— night sky red with the promise of fortune,
dawn pink as new flesh: healing, unfettered.

JANUARY 1863

Today, dawn red as warning. Unfettered
supplies, stacked on the beach at our landing,
washed away in the storm that rose too fast,
caught us unprepared. Later, as we worked,
I joined in the low singing someone raised
to pace us, and felt a bond in labor
I had not known. It was then a dark man
removed his shirt, revealed the scars, crosshatched
like the lines in this journal, on his back.
It was he who remarked at how the ropes
cracked like whips on the sand, made us take note
of the wild dance of a tent loosed by wind.
We watched and learned. Like any shrewd master,
we know now to tie down what we will keep.

FEBRUARY 1863

We know it is our duty now to keep
white men as prisoners — rebel soldiers,
would-be masters. We're all bondsmen here, each
to the other. Freedom has gotten them
captivity. For us, a conscription
we have chosen — jailors to those who still
would have us slaves. They are cautious, dreading
the sight of us. Some neither read nor write,
are laid too low and have few words to send
but those I give them. Still, they are wary
of a negro writing, taking down letters.

X binds them to the page—a mute symbol
like the cross on a grave. I suspect they fear
I'll listen, put something else down in ink.

MARCH 1863

I listen, put down in ink what I know
they labor to say between silences
too big for words: worry for beloveds—
My Dearest, how are you getting along—
what has become of their small plots of land—
did you harvest enough food to put by?
They long for the comfort of former lives—
I see you as you were, waving goodbye.
Some send photographs—a likeness in case
the body can't return. Others dictate
harsh facts of this war: *The hot air carries*
the stench of limbs, rotten in the bone pit.
Flies swarm—a black cloud. We hunger, grow weak.
When men die, we eat their share of hardtack.

APRIL 1863

When men die, we eat their share of hardtack
trying not to recall their hollow sockets,
the worm-stitch of their cheeks. Today we buried
the last of our dead from Pascagoula,
and those who died retreating to our ship—

white sailors in blue firing upon us
as if we were the enemy. I'd thought
the fighting over, then watched a man fall
beside me, knees-first as in prayer, then
another, his arms outstretched as if borne
upon the cross. Smoke that rose from each gun
seemed a soul departing. The Colonel said:
an unfortunate incident; said:
their names shall deck the page of history.

JUNE 1863

Some names shall deck the page of history
as it is written on stone. Some will not.
Yesterday, word came of colored troops, dead
on the battlefield at Port Hudson; how
General Banks was heard to say *I have*
no dead there, and left them, unclaimed. Last night,
I dreamt their eyes still open — dim, clouded
as the eyes of fish washed ashore, yet fixed —
staring back at me. Still, more come today
eager to enlist. Their bodies — haggard
faces, gaunt limbs — bring news of the mainland.
Starved, they suffer like our prisoners. Dying,
they plead for what we do not have to give.
Death makes equals of us all: a fair master.

AUGUST 1864

Dumas was a fair master to us all.
He taught me to read and write: I was a man-
servant, if not a man. At my work,
I studied natural things—all manner
of plants, birds I draw now in my book: wren,
willet, egret, loon. Tending the gardens,
I thought only to study live things, thought
never to know so much about the dead.
Now I tend Ship Island graves, mounds like dunes
that shift and disappear. I record names,
send home simple notes, not much more than how
and when—an official duty. I'm told
it's best to spare most detail, but I know
there are things which must be accounted for.

1865

These are things which must be accounted for:
slaughter under the white flag of surrender—
black massacre at Fort Pillow; our new name,
the Corps d'Afrique—words that take the *native*
from our claim; mossbacks and freedmen—exiles
in their own homeland; the diseased, the maimed,
every lost limb, and what remains: phantom
ache, memory haunting an empty sleeve;

the hog-eaten at Gettysburg, unmarked
in their graves; all the dead letters, unanswered;
untold stories of those that time will render
mute. Beneath battlefields, green again,
the dead molder — a scaffolding of bone
we tread upon, forgetting. Truth be told.

Again, the Fields

AFTER WINSLOW HOMER

the dead they lay long the lines like sheaves of Wheat I could
have walked on the boddes all most from one end too the other

No more muskets, the bone-drag
weariness of marching, the trampled
grass, soaked earth red as the wine

of sacrament. Now, the veteran
turns toward a new field, bright
as domes of the republic. Here,

he has shrugged off the past — his jacket
and canteen flung down in the corner.
At the center of the painting, he anchors

the trinity, joining earth and sky.
The wheat falls beneath his scythe —
a language of bounty — the swaths

like scripture on the field's open page.
Boundless, the wheat stretches beyond
the frame, as if toward a distant field —

the white canvas where sky and cotton
meet, where another veteran toils,
his hands the color of dark soil.

III

O magnet-South! O glistening perfumed South! my South!
O quick mettle, rich blood, impulse and love! good and evil! O all
*   dear to me!*

—Walt Whitman

Pastoral

In the dream, I am with the Fugitive
Poets. We're gathered for a photograph.
Behind us, the skyline of Atlanta
hidden by the photographer's backdrop—
a lush pasture, green, full of soft-eyed cows
lowing, a chant that sounds like *no, no. Yes,*
I say to the glass of bourbon I'm offered.
We're lining up now—Robert Penn Warren,
his voice just audible above the drone
of bulldozers, telling us where to stand.
Say "race," the photographer croons. I'm in
blackface again when the flash freezes us.
My father's white, I tell them, *and rural.*
You don't hate the South? they ask. *You don't hate it?*

Miscegenation

In 1965 my parents broke two laws of Mississippi;
they went to Ohio to marry, returned to Mississippi.

They crossed the river into Cincinnati, a city whose name
begins with a sound like *sin,* the sound of wrong — *mis* in Mississippi.

A year later they moved to Canada, followed a route the same
as slaves, the train slicing the white glaze of winter, leaving Mississippi.

Faulkner's Joe Christmas was born in winter, like Jesus, given his name
for the day he was left at the orphanage, his race unknown in Mississippi.

My father was reading *War and Peace* when he gave me my name.
I was born near Easter, 1966, in Mississippi.

When I turned 33 my father said, *It's your Jesus year — you're the same
age he was when he died.* It was spring, the hills green in Mississippi.

I know more than Joe Christmas did. Natasha is a Russian name —
though I'm not; it means *Christmas child,* even in Mississippi.

My Mother Dreams Another Country

Already the words are changing. She is changing
    from *colored* to *negro, black* still years ahead.
This is 1966 — she is married to a white man —
    and there are more names for what grows inside her.
It is enough to worry about words like *mongrel*
    and the infertility of mules and *mulattoes*
while flipping through a book of baby names.
    She has come home to wait out the long months,
her room unchanged since she's been gone:
    dolls winking down from every shelf — all of them
white. Every day she is flanked by the rituals of superstition,
    and there is a name she will learn for this too:
maternal impression — the shape, like an unknown
    country, marking the back of the newborn's thigh.
For now, women tell her to clear her head, to steady her hands
    or she'll gray a lock of the child's hair wherever
she worries her own, imprint somewhere the outline
    of a thing she craves too much. They tell her
to stanch her cravings by eating dirt. All spring
    she has sat on her hands, her fingers numb. For a while
each day, she can't feel anything she touches: the arbor
    out back — the landscape's green tangle; the molehill
of her own swelling. Here — outside the city limits —
    cars speed by, clouds of red dust in their wake.
She breathes it in — *Mississippi* — then drifts toward sleep,
    thinking of someplace she's never been. Late,

Mississippi is a dark backdrop bearing down
        on the windows of her room. On the TV in the corner,
the station signs off, broadcasting its nightly salutation:
        the waving Stars and Stripes, our national anthem.

Southern History

Before the war, they were happy, he said,
quoting our textbook. (This was senior-year

history class.) *The slaves were clothed, fed,*
and better off under a master's care.

I watched the words blur on the page. No one
raised a hand, disagreed. Not even me.

It was late; we still had Reconstruction
to cover before the test, and — luckily —

three hours of watching *Gone with the Wind.*
History, the teacher said, *of the old South —*

a true account of how things were back then.
On screen a slave stood big as life: big mouth,

bucked eyes, our textbook's grinning proof — a lie
my teacher guarded. Silent, so did I.

Blond

Certainly it was possible — somewhere
in my parents' genes the recessive traits
that might have given me a different look:
not attached earlobes or my father's green eyes,
but another hair color — gentleman-preferred,
have-more-fun blond. And with my skin color,
like a good tan — an even mix of my parents' —
I could have passed for white.

When on Christmas day I woke to find
a blond wig, a pink sequined tutu,
and a blond ballerina doll, nearly tall as me,
I didn't know to ask, nor that it mattered,
if there'd been a brown version. This was years before
my grandmother nestled the dark baby
into our crèche, years before I'd understand it
as primer for a Mississippi childhood.

Instead, I pranced around our living room
in a whirl of possibility, my parents looking on
at their suddenly strange child. In the photograph
my mother took, my father — almost
out of the frame — looks on as Joseph must have
at the miraculous birth: I'm in the foreground —
my blond wig a shining halo, a newborn likeness
to the child that chance, the long odds,
might have brought.

Southern Gothic

I have lain down into 1970, into the bed
my parents will share for only a few more years.
Early evening, they have not yet turned from each other
in sleep, their bodies curved — parentheses
framing the separate lives they'll wake to. Dreaming,
I am again the child with too many questions —
the endless *why* and *why* and *why*
my mother cannot answer, her mouth closed, a gesture
toward her future: cold lips stitched shut.
The lines in my young father's face deepen
toward an expression of grief. I have come home
from the schoolyard with the words that shadow us
in this small Southern town — *peckerwood* and *nigger
lover, half-breed* and *zebra* — words that take shape
outside us. We're huddled on the tiny island of bed, quiet
in the language of blood: the house, unsteady
on its cinderblock haunches, sinking deeper
into the muck of ancestry. Oil lamps flicker
around us — our shadows, dark glyphs on the wall,
bigger and stranger than we are.

Incident

We tell the story every year —
how we peered from the windows, shades drawn —
though nothing really happened,
the charred grass now green again.

We peered from the windows, shades drawn,
at the cross trussed like a Christmas tree,
the charred grass still green. Then
we darkened our rooms, lit the hurricane lamps.

At the cross trussed like a Christmas tree,
a few men gathered, white as angels in their gowns.
We darkened our rooms and lit hurricane lamps,
the wicks trembling in their fonts of oil.

It seemed the angels had gathered, white men in their gowns.
When they were done, they left quietly. No one came.
The wicks trembled all night in their fonts of oil;
by morning the flames had all dimmed.

When they were done, the men left quietly. No one came.
Nothing really happened.
By morning all the flames had dimmed.
We tell the story every year.

Providence

What's left is footage: the hours before
      Camille, 1969 — hurricane
            parties, palm trees leaning
in the wind,
      fronds blown back,

a woman's hair. Then after:
      the vacant lots,
        boats washed ashore, a swamp

where graves had been. I recall

how we huddled all night in our small house,
      moving between rooms,
            emptying pots filled with rain.

The next day, our house —
      on its cinderblocks — seemed to float

      in the flooded yard: no foundation

beneath us, nothing I could see
         tying us   to the land.
         In the water, our reflection
                trembled,
disappeared
when I bent to touch it.

Monument

Today the ants are busy
   beside my front steps, weaving
in and out of the hill they're building.
   I watch them emerge and—

like everything I've forgotten—disappear
   into the subterranean—a world
made by displacement. In the cemetery
   last June, I circled, lost—

weeds and grass grown up all around—
   the landscape blurred and waving.
At my mother's grave, ants streamed in
   and out like arteries, a tiny hill rising

above her untended plot. Bit by bit,
   red dirt piled up, spread
like a rash on the grass; I watched a long time
   the ants' determined work,

how they brought up soil
   of which she will be part,
and piled it before me. Believe me when I say
   I've tried not to begrudge them

their industry, this reminder of what
    I haven't done. Even now,
the mound is a blister on my heart,
    a red and humming swarm.

Elegy for the Native Guards

Now that the salt of their blood
Stiffens the saltier oblivion of the sea . . .

— Allen Tate

We leave Gulfport at noon; gulls overhead
trailing the boat — streamers, noisy fanfare —
all the way to Ship Island. What we see
first is the fort, its roof of grass, a lee —
half reminder of the men who served there —
a weathered monument to some of the dead.

Inside we follow the ranger, hurried
though we are to get to the beach. He tells
of graves lost in the Gulf, the island split
in half when Hurricane Camille hit,
shows us casemates, cannons, the store that sells
souvenirs, tokens of history long buried.

The Daughters of the Confederacy
has placed a plaque here, at the fort's entrance —
each Confederate soldier's name raised hard
in bronze; no names carved for the Native Guards —
2nd Regiment, Union men, black phalanx.
What is monument to their legacy?

All the grave markers, all the crude headstones —
water-lost. Now fish dart among their bones,
and we listen for what the waves intone.
Only the fort remains, near forty feet high,
round, unfinished, half open to the sky,
the elements — wind, rain — God's deliberate eye.

South

Homo sapiens *is the only species to suffer psychological exile.*
    —E. O. Wilson

I returned to a stand of pines,
                bone-thin phalanx

flanking the roadside, tangle
                of understory—a dialectic of dark

and light—and magnolias blossoming
                like afterthought: each flower

a surrender, white flags draped
                among the branches. I returned

to land's end, the swath of coast
                clear cut and buried in sand:

mangrove, live oak, gulfweed
                razed and replaced by thin palms—

palmettos—symbols of victory
                or defiance, over and over

marking this vanquished land. I returned
                to a field of cotton, hallowed ground—

as slave legend goes — each boll
　　　　　holding the ghosts of generations:

those who measured their days
　　　　　by the heft of sacks and lengths

of rows, whose sweat flecked the cotton plants
　　　　　still sewn into our clothes.

I returned to a country battlefield
　　　　　where colored troops fought and died —

Port Hudson where their bodies swelled
　　　　　and blackened beneath the sun — unburied

until earth's green sheet pulled over them,
　　　　　unmarked by any headstones.

Where the roads, buildings, and monuments
　　　　　are named to honor the Confederacy,

where that old flag still hangs, I return
　　　　　to Mississippi, state that made a crime

of me — mulatto, half-breed — native
　　　　　in my native land, this place they'll bury me.

IV

from

CONGREGATION

Invocation, 1926

How they rose early, a list of chores
pulling them toward the kitchen
in dim light — work that must be done
before the rest of their work be done.

How they walked for miles, down
the Gulf and Ship Island Line, toward
the beach, through the quarters, beyond
shotgun shacks, and into the city limits

where white children stood guard — sentries
on a section of rail — muscling them off
the tracks. How they walked on anyway,
until they waded into water, neck-deep,

though they could not swim — a baptism —
something akin to faith, the daily catch
keeping them afloat. How they tied the lines,
walked back and forth to find each cluster,

each glorious net of crabs. Across sand, the road
hot beneath their feet, then door to back door
they went, my grandmother and her siblings,
knocking, offering their catch, cleaned first

on the back steps, gutted—a display of yellow
bright as sunshine raining down on the grass.
When my grandmother prepared crabs for me
I saw the girl she once was, her nimble hands,

food on the table in all those alien houses
along the beach. On our table: crabs, a mound
of rice steaming in a bowl, gumbo manna—
the line between us and them, between the whites

on one side of the tracks, us on the other, sure
as the crab lines she set, the work of her hands,
that which sustains us. Lord, bless those hands,
the harvesters. Bless the travelers who gather

our food, and those who grow it, clean it, cook it,
who bring it to our tables. Bless the laborers
whose faces we do not see—like the girl
my grandmother was, walking the rails home:

bless us that we remember.

Congregation

Believe the report of the Lord /
Face the things that confront you.

      —marquee (front / back),
      Greater Mt. Rest Baptist Church,
      Gulfport, Mississippi, May 2009

1. WITNESS

Here is North Gulfport—
its liquor stores and car washes,
trailers and shotgun shacks
propped at the road's edge;
its brick houses hunkered
against the weather, anchored
to neat, clipped yards;
its streets named for states
and Presidents—each corner
a crossroads of memory,
marked with a white obelisk;
its phalanx of church houses—
a congregation of bunkers
and masonry brick, chorus
of marquees: *God is not*
the author of fear; Without faith
we is victims; Sooner or later
everybody comes by here.

2. WATCHER

AFTER KATRINA, 2005

At first, there was nothing to do but watch.
For days, before the trucks arrived, before the work
of clean-up, my brother sat on the stoop and watched.

He watched the ambulances speed by, the police cars;
watched for the looters who'd come each day
to siphon gas from the car, take away the generator,

the air conditioner, whatever there was to be had.
He watched his phone for a signal, watched the sky
for signs of a storm, for rain so he could wash.

At the church, handing out diapers and water,
he watched the people line up, watched their faces
as they watched his. And when at last there was work,

he got a job, on the beach, as a *watcher*.
Behind safety goggles, he watched the sand for bones,
searched for debris that clogged the great machines.

Riding the prow of the cleaners, or walking ahead,
he watched for carcasses — chickens mostly, maybe
some cats or dogs. No one said *remains*. No one

had to. It was a kind of faith, that watching:
my brother trained his eyes to bear
the sharp erasure of sand and glass, prayed

there'd be nothing more to see.

3. BELIEVER

FOR TAMARA JONES

The house is in need of repair, but is—
for now, she says—still hers. After the storm
she laid hands on what she could reclaim:
the iron table and chairs etched with rust,
the dresser laced with mold. Four years gone,
she's still rebuilding the shed out back
and sorting through boxes in the kitchen—
a lifetime of bills and receipts, deeds
and warranties, notices spread on the table,
a barrage of red ink: PAST DUE. Now
the house is a museum of everything

she can't let go: a pile of photographs—
fused and peeling—water stains blurring
the handwritten names of people she can't recall;
a drawer crowded with funeral programs
and church fans, rubber bands and paper sleeves
for pennies, nickels, and dimes. What stops me
is the stack of tithing envelopes. Reading my face,
she must know I can't see why—even now—
she tithes, why she keeps giving to the church.
First seek the kingdom of God, she tells me,
and the rest will follow—says it twice

as if to make a talisman of her words.

4. KIN

FOR ROY LEE JEFFERSON

He has the surname that suggests
a contested kinship: *Jefferson* —
the name, too, of this dead-end street
cut in half by Highway 49. Here,
at the corner where it crosses Alabama,
he's perched on the stoop, early evening,
at my cousin Tammy's house, empty
bottles at his feet. When he sees me
opening the gate, walking up smiling,
he reads me first as *white woman,* then —
he says — *half-breed.* It's my hair, he tells me:
No black woman got hair like that,
and my car, a sedan he insists
the cops don't let black people drive,
not here, not without pulling them over
again and again. He's still wearing
his work uniform — grass stains and clippings
from the mower he pushed all day —
and his name tag, a badge, still pinned
to his collar. He tells me he'd swap the badge
for one from another boss, switch jobs
if he could get more pay; says
his boss has plenty of money — *cheese,*
he calls it. *Man's tight with it, he squeak
when he walk.* So Roy waits, biding
his time, he says, *till the Lord bless me
with something else.* When he goes quiet,
I ask him the easy question — one I know

he's been asked a hundred times —
just to hear him talk: *Where were you*
during the storm? That's when he tells me
what he hasn't this whole time, holding it back
maybe, saving it for the right moment:
I got a baby with your cousin Tammy's sister —
that makes us kin. You can't run
from the Lord. I don't know what he sees
in my face, but he grins at me, nodding.
White girl, he says, *you gone come*
see my baby, come up to the country
where we stay? He's walking away now,
a tallboy in his hand. I'm trying to say
yes, one day, sure, but he's nearly gone,
looking back over his shoulder, shaking
his head, laughing now as he says this:
When you waiting on kinfolks,
you be waiting forever.

5. EXEGESIS

On Saturday, when I come to see
my brother, they call him over loudspeaker
to the *tower*—a small guardroom
at the entrance to the prison. I sign my name
in the book, write R0470—his number—
and agree to a search. I stand as if
I would make a snow angel in the air,
and the woman guard pats me down
lightly. Waiting for him, I consider

the squat room's title: how it once meant
prison, and to the religious faithful, *heaven.*
Here, my brother has no use for these words,
this easy parsing. This time he tells me
he's changed his name: Jo-ell instead of Joel—
name of the man who took our mother's life—
his father, an inmate somewhere else.
Thinking only of words, I'd wanted to tell him
the name means *prophet.* That was before I knew

it had—for him—been a prison, too.

6. PRODIGAL

I

Once, I was a daughter of this place:
daughter of Gwen, granddaughter
of Leretta, great- of Eugenia McGee.

I was baptized in the church
my great-aunt founded, behind
the drapes my grandmother sewed.

As a child, I dozed in the pews
and woke to chant the Lord's Prayer —
mouthing the lines I did not learn.

Still a girl, I put down the red flower
and wore a white bloom pinned to my chest —
the mark of loss: a motherless child. All

the elders knew who I was, recalled me
each time I came home and spoke
my ancestors' names — Sugar, Son Dixon —

a native tongue. What is home but a cradle
of the past? Too long gone, I've found
my key in the lock of the old house

will not turn — a narrative of rust;
and everywhere the lacunae of vacant lots,
For Sale signs, a notice reading *Condemned*.

II

I wanted to say I have come home
to bear witness, to read the sign
emblazoned on the church marquee —
Believe the report of the Lord —
and trust that this is noble work, that
which must be done. I wanted to say *I see,*
not *I watch.* I wanted my seeing to be
a sanctuary, but what I saw was this:
in my rearview mirror, the marquee's
other side — *Face the things that confront you.*

My first day back, a pilgrim, I traveled
the old neighborhood, windows up,
steering the car down streets I hadn't seen
in years. It was Sunday. At the rebuilt church
across from my grandmother's house,
I stepped into the vestibule and found
not a solid wall as years before, but
a new wall, glass through which I could see
the sanctuary. And so, I did not go in;
I stood there, my face against the glass,

watching. I could barely hear the organ,
the hymn they sang, but when the congregation rose,
filing out of the pews, I knew it was the call
to altar. And still, I did not enter. Outside,
as I'd lingered at the car, a man had said,

You got to come in. You can't miss the word.
I got as far as the vestibule — neither in
nor out. The service went on. I did nothing
but watch, my face against the glass — until
someone turned, looked back: saw me.

7. BENEDICTION

I thought that when I saw my brother
walking through the gates of the prison,
he would look like a man entering

his life. And he did. He carried
a small bag, holding it away from his body
as if he would not touch it, or

that it weighed almost nothing.
The clothes he wore seemed to belong
to someone else, like hand-me-downs

given a child who will one day
grow into them. Behind him, at the fence,
the inmates were waving, someone saying

All right now. And then
my brother was walking toward us,
a few awkward steps, at first, until

he got it — how to hold up the too-big pants
with one hand, and in the other
carry everything else he had.

Liturgy

FOR THE MISSISSIPPI GULF COAST

To the security guard staring at the Gulf
thinking of bodies washed away from the coast, plugging her ears
against the bells and sirens — sound of alarm — the gaming floor
on the Coast;

To Billy Scarpetta, waiting tables on the Coast, staring at the Gulf
thinking of water rising, thinking of New Orleans, thinking of cleansing
the Coast;

To the woman dreaming of returning to the Coast, thinking of water
     rising,
her daughter's grave, my mother's grave — underwater — on the Coast;

To Miss Mary, somewhere;

To the displaced, living in trailers along the coast, beside the highway,
in vacant lots and open fields; to everyone who stayed on the Coast,
who came back — or cannot — to the Coast;

For those who died on the Coast.

This is a memory of the Coast: to each his own
recollections, her reclamations, their
restorations, the return of the Coast.

This is a time capsule for the Coast: words of the people
—*don't forget us*—
the sound of wind, waves, the silence of graves,
the muffled voice of history, bulldozed and buried
under sand poured on the eroding coast,
the concrete slabs of rebuilding the Coast.

This is a love letter to the Gulf Coast, a praise song, a dirge,
invocation and benediction, a requiem for the Gulf Coast.

This cannot rebuild the Coast; it is an indictment, a complaint,
my *logos*—argument and discourse—with the Coast.

This is my *nostos*—my pilgrimage to the Coast, my memory,
    my reckoning—

native daughter: I am the Gulf Coast.

V

from

THRALL

What is love?
One name for it is knowledge.

  —Robert Penn Warren

After such knowledge, what forgiveness?

  —T. S. Eliot

Illumination

Always   there is something more to know
    what lingers   at the edge of thought
awaiting illumination   as in
    this secondhand book   full
of annotations   daring the margins in pencil
a light stroke as if
    the writer of these small replies
meant not to leave them   forever
    meant to erase
evidence of this private interaction
    Here   a passage underlined   there
a single star on the page
    as in a night sky   cloud-swept and hazy
where only the brightest appears
    a tiny spark   I follow
its coded message   try to read in it
the direction of the solitary mind
    that thought to pencil in
a jagged arrow   It
    is a bolt of lightning
where it strikes
    I read the line over and over
as if I might discern
    the little fires set
the flames of an idea   licking the page
how knowledge burns   Beyond
    the exclamation point
its thin agreement   angle of surprise

there are questions   the word *why*

So much is left

    untold   Between

the printed words   and the self-conscious scrawl

    between   what is said and not

white space framing the story

    the way the past   unwritten

eludes us   So much

    is implication   the afterimage

of measured syntax   always there

    ghosting the margins that words

their black-lined authority

    do not cross   Even

as they rise up   to meet us

    the white page hovers beneath

silent   incendiary   waiting

Knowledge

AFTER A CHALK DRAWING BY

J. H. HASSELHORST, 1864

Whoever she was, she comes to us like this:
 lips parted, long hair spilling from the table

like water from a pitcher, nipples drawn out
 for inspection. Perhaps to foreshadow

the object she'll become: a skeleton on a pedestal,
 a row of skulls on a shelf. To make a study

of the ideal female body, four men gather around her.
 She is young and beautiful and drowned—

a Venus de' Medici, risen from the sea, sleeping.
 As if we could mistake this work for sacrilege,

the artist entombs her body in a pyramid
 of light, a temple of science over which

the anatomist presides. In the service of beauty—
 to know it—he lifts a flap of skin

beneath her breast as one might draw back a sheet.
 We will not see his step-by-step parsing,

a translation: *Mary* or *Katherine* or *Elizabeth*
    to *corpus, areola, vulva.* In his hands

instruments of the empirical—scalpel, pincers—
    cold as the room must be cold: all the men

in coats, trimmed in velvet or fur—soft as the down
    of her pubis. Now one man is smoking, another

tilts his head to get a better look. Yet another,
    at the head of the table, peers down as if

enthralled, his fist on a stack of books.
    In the drawing this is only the first cut,

a delicate wounding; and yet how easily
    the anatomist's blade opens a place in me,

like a curtain drawn upon a room in which
    each learned man is my father

and I hear, again, his words—*I study*
    my crossbreed child—misnomer

and taxonomy, the language of zoology. Here,
    he is all of them: the preoccupied man—

an artist, collector of experience; the skeptic angling
    his head, his thoughts tilting toward

what I cannot know; the marshaller of knowledge,
     knuckling down a stack of books; even

the dissector — his scalpel in hand like a pen
     poised above me, aimed straight for my heart.

Miracle of the Black Leg

PICTORIAL REPRESENTATIONS OF PHYSICIAN-
SAINTS COSMAS AND DAMIAN AND THE MYTH OF
THE MIRACLE TRANSPLANT — BLACK DONOR,
WHITE RECIPIENT — DATE BACK TO THE
MID-FOURTEENTH CENTURY, APPEARING MUCH
LATER THAN WRITTEN VERSIONS OF THE STORY.

1

Always, the dark body hewn asunder; always
    one man is healed, his sick limb replaced,
placed in the other man's grave: the white leg
    buried beside the corpse or attached as if
it were always there. If not for the dark appendage
    you might miss the story beneath this story—
what remains each time the myth changes: how,
    in one version, the doctors harvest the leg
from a man, four days dead, in his tomb at the church
    of a martyr, or—in another—desecrate a body
fresh in the graveyard at Saint Peter in Chains:
    There was buried just today an Ethiopian.
Even now, it stays with us: when we mean to uncover
    the truth, we dig, say *unearth*.

2

Emblematic in paint, a signifier of the body's lacuna,
    the black leg is at once a grafted narrative,
a redacted line of text, and in this scene a dark stocking
    pulled above the knee. Here the patient sleeping,
his head at rest in his hand. Beatific, he looks as if
    he'll wake from a dream. On the floor
beside the bed, a dead *Moor*—hands crossed at the groin,
    the swapped limb white and rotting, fused in place.
And in the corner, a question: poised as if to speak
    the syntax of sloughing, a snake's curved form.
It emerges from the mouth of a boy like a tongue—slippery
    and rooted in the body as knowledge. For centuries
this is how the myth repeats: the miracle—in words
    or wood or paint—is a record of thought.

3

See how the story changes: in one painting
    the *Ethiop* is merely a body, featureless in a coffin,
so black he has no face. In another, the patient—
    at the top of the frame—seems to writhe in pain,
the black leg grafted to his thigh. Below him
    a mirror of suffering: the *blackamoor*—
his body a fragment—arched across the doctor's lap
    as if dying from his wound. If not immanence,
the soul's bright anchor, blood passed from one
    to the other, what knowledge haunts each body—
what history, what phantom ache? One man always
    low, in a grave or on the ground, the other
up high, closer to heaven; one man always diseased,
    the other a body in service, plundered.

4

Both men are alive in Villoldo's carving.
    In twinned relief, they hold the same posture,
the same pained face, each man reaching to touch
      his left leg. The black man, on the floor,
holds his stump. Above him, the doctor restrains
      the patient's arm as if to prevent him touching
the dark amendment of flesh. How not to see it—
      the men bound one to the other, symbiotic—
one man rendered expendable, the other worthy
      of this sacrifice? In version after version, even
when the *Ethiopian* isn't there, the leg is a stand-in,
      a black modifier against the white body,
a piece cut off—as in the origin of the word *comma:*
      caesura in a story that's still being written.

The Americans

1. DR. SAMUEL ADOLPHUS CARTWRIGHT ON DISSECTING THE WHITE NEGRO, 1851

To strip from the flesh
    the specious skin; to weigh
      in the brainpan
    seeds of white
pepper; to find in the body
    its own diminishment —
      blood-deep
    and definite; to measure the heft
of lack; to make of the work of faith
    the work of science, evidence
      the word of God: Canaan
be the *servant of servants;* thus
    to know the truth
      of this: (this derelict
corpus, a dark compendium, this
    atavistic assemblage — flatter
feet, bowed legs, a shorter neck) so
    deep the tincture
      — *see it!* —
we still know white from not.

2. BLOOD

AFTER GEORGE FULLER'S *The Quadroon,* 1880

It must be the gaze of a benevolent viewer
upon her, framed as she is in the painting's
romantic glow, her melancholic beauty
meant to show the pathos of her condition:
black blood—that she cannot transcend it.
In the foreground she is shown at rest, seated,
her basket empty and overturned beside her
as though she would cast down the drudgery
to which she was born. A gleaner, hopeless
undine—the bucolic backdrop a dim aura
around her—she looks out toward us as if
to bridge the distance between. *Mezzo,*
intermediate, how different she's rendered
from the dark kin working the fields behind her.
If not for the ray of light appearing as if from beyond
the canvas, we might miss them—three figures
in the near distance, small as afterthought.

3. HELP, 1968

AFTER A PHOTOGRAPH FROM *The Americans*
BY ROBERT FRANK

When I see Frank's photograph
of a white infant in the dark arms
of a woman who must be the maid,
I think of my mother and the year
we spent alone — my father at sea.

The woman stands in profile, back
against a wall, holding her charge,
their faces side by side — the look
on the child's face strangely prescient,
a tiny furrow in the space
between her brows. Neither of them
looks toward the camera; nor
do they look at each other. That year,

when my mother took me for walks,
she was mistaken again and again
for my maid. Years later she told me
she'd say I was her daughter, and each time
strangers would stare in disbelief, then
empty the change from their pockets. Now

I think of the betrayals of flesh, how
she must have tried to make of her face
an inscrutable mask and hold it there
as they made their small offerings —
pressing coins into my hands. How

like the woman in the photograph
she must have seemed, carrying me
each day — white in her arms — as if
she were a prop: a black backdrop,
the dark foil in this American story.

Taxonomy

AFTER A SERIES OF *casta* PAINTINGS
BY JUAN RODRÍGUEZ JUÁREZ, C. 1715

1. *DE ESPAÑOL Y DE INDIA PRODUCE MESTISO*

The canvas is a leaden sky
    behind them, heavy
with words, gold letters inscribing
    an equation of blood —

this plus this equals this — as if
    a contract with nature, or
a museum label,
    ethnographic, precise. See

how the father's hand, beneath
    its crown of lace,
curls around his daughter's head;
    she's nearly fair

as he is — *calidad*. See it
    in the brooch at her collar,
the lace framing her face.
    An infant, she is borne

over the servant's left shoulder,
    bound to him
by a sling, the plain blue cloth
    knotted at his throat.

If the father, his hand
    on her skull, divines —
as the physiognomist does —
    the mysteries

of her character, discursive,
    legible on her light flesh,
in the soft curl of her hair,
    we cannot know it: so gentle

the eye he turns toward her.
    The mother, glancing
sideways toward him —
    the scarf on her head

white as his face,
    his powdered wig — gestures
with one hand a shape
    like the letter C. *See,*

she seems to say,
    what we have made.
The servant, still a child, cranes
    his neck, turns his face

up toward all of them. He is dark
    as history, origin of the word
native: the weight of blood,
    a pale mistress on his back,

heavier every year.

2. DE ESPAÑOL Y NEGRA PRODUCE MULATO

Still, the centuries have not dulled
the sullenness of the child's expression.

If there is light inside him, it does not shine
through the paint that holds his face

in profile—his domed forehead, eyes
nearly closed beneath a heavy brow.

Though inside, the boy's father stands
in his cloak and hat. It's as if he's just come in,

or that he's leaving. We see him
transient, rolling a cigarette, myopic—

his eyelids drawn against the child
passing before him. At the stove,

the boy's mother contorts, watchful,
her neck twisting on its spine, red beads

yoked at her throat like a necklace of blood,
her face so black she nearly disappears

into the canvas, the dark wall upon which
we see the words that name them.

What should we make of any of this?
Remove the words above their heads,

put something else in place of the child —
a table, perhaps, upon which the man might set

his hat, or a dog upon which to bestow
the blessing of his touch — and the story

changes. The boy is a palimpsest of paint —
layers of color, history rendering him

that precise shade of in-between.
Before this he was nothing: blank

canvas — before image or word, before
a last brush stroke fixed him in his place.

3. DE ESPAÑOL Y MESTIZA PRODUCE CASTIZA

How not to see
    in this gesture

the mind
    of the colony?

In the mother's arms,
    the child, hinged

at her womb—
    dark cradle

of mixed blood
    (call it *Mexico*)—

turns toward the father,
    reaching to him

as if back to Spain,
    to the promise of blood

alchemy—three easy steps
    to purity:

from a Spaniard and an Indian,
    a mestizo;

from a mestizo and a Spaniard,
    a castizo;

from a castizo and a Spaniard,
    a Spaniard.

We see her here —
    one generation away —

nearly slipping
    her mother's careful grip.

4. THE BOOK OF CASTAS

Call it the catalog
    of mixed bloods, or

        the book of naught:
            not Spaniard, not white, but

mulatto-returning-backwards (or
    hold-yourself-in-midair) and

        the *morisca,* the *lobo,* the *chino,*
            sambo, albino, and

the *no-te-entiendo* — the
    I don't understand you.

        Guidebook to the colony,
            record of each crossed birth,

it is the typology of taint,
    of stain: blemish: sullying spot:

        that which can be purified,
            that which cannot — Canaan's

black fate. How like a dirty joke
    it seems: *What do you call*

        that space between
            the dark geographies of sex?

Call it the *taint* — as in
　　　T'aint one and t'aint the other —

illicit and yet naming still
　　　what is between. Between

her parents, the child,
　　　mulatto-returning-backwards,

cannot slip their hold,
　　　the triptych their bodies make

in paint, in blood: her name
　　　written down in the *Book*

　　of Castas — all her kind
　　　in thrall to a word.

Thrall

He was not my father
though   he might have been
    I came to him
the mulatto son
        of a slave woman
    just that
as if   it took only my mother
    to make me
        a *mulatto*
meaning
    any white man
could be my father

            ❖

In his shop   bound
    to the muller
I ground his colors
    my hands dusted   black
with fired bone   stained
    blue   and flecked
with glass   my nails
edged vermilion   as if
    my fingertips bled
In this way   just as
    I'd turned the pages
of his books

I meant to touch
    everything he did

   ❖

With Velázquez   in Rome
    a divination
At market   I lingered to touch
    the bright hulls of lemons
        closed my eyes until
    the scent was oil
and thinner   yellow ocher
    in my head
        And once
the sudden taste of iron
        a glimpse of red
    like a wound opening
        the robes of the pope
at portrait
    that bright shade of blood
        before it darkens
purpling nearly to black

   ❖

Because he said
    painting was not
    labor   was
the province of free men
    I could only
watch   Such beauty
    in the work of his hands
        his quick strokes
        a divine language I learned

over his shoulder
      my own hands
tracing the air
     in his wake   Forbidden
        to answer in paint
I kept my canvases secret
      hidden until
     Velázquez decreed
       unto me
    myself   Free
I was apprentice   he
      my master still

    ❖

How intently at times
     could he fix his keen eye
       upon me
though only once
     did he fix me   in paint
my color a study
    my eyes wide
      as I faced him
a lace collar at my shoulders
     as though I'd been born
       noble
    the yoke of my birth
gone from my neck
     In his hand   a long brush
       to keep him far
     from the canvas
far from it   as I was

                    the distance between us
                        doubled   that
he could observe me
            twice   stand closer
                    to what *he* made
For years   I looked to it
            as one looks into a mirror

            ❖

                    And so
in *The Calling of Saint Matthew*
            I painted my own
likeness   a freeman
            in the House of Customs
                        waiting to pay
my duty   In my hand
            an answer   a slip of paper
                    my signature on it
            Juan de Pareja   1661
Velázquez   one year gone
            Behind me
                    upright on a shelf
a forged platter   luminous
                    as an aureole
            just beyond my head
                    my face turned
to look out from the scene
            a self portrait
To make it
                    I looked at how
my master saw me   then
            I narrowed my eyes

❖

Now
    at the bright edge
of sleep   *mother*
She comes back to me
    as sound
      her voice
in the echo of birdcall
    a single syllable
      again
and again   my name
    Juan Juan Juan
or   a bit of song   that
      waking
I cannot grasp

Calling

MEXICO, 1969

Why not make a fiction
        of the mind's fictions? I want to say
    it begins like this: the trip
            a pilgrimage, my mother
kneeling at the altar of the Black Virgin,
        enthralled — light streaming in
            a window, the sun
        at her back, holy water
    in a bowl she must have touched.

What's left is palimpsest — one memory
    bleeding into another, overwriting it.
        How else to explain
            what remains? The sound
    of water in a basin I know is white,
        the sun behind her, light streaming in,
            her face —
    as if she were already dead — blurred
        as it will become.

I want to imagine her before
    the altar, rising to meet us, my father
        lifting me
      toward her outstretched arms.
    What else to make
      of the mind's slick confabulations?
      What comes back
is the sun's dazzle on a pool's surface,
      light filtered through water

closing over my head, my mother—her body
    between me and the high sun, a corona of light
      around her face. Why not call it
    a vision? What I know is this:
I was drowning and saw a dark Madonna;
      someone pulled me through
    the water's bright ceiling
      and I rose, initiate,
    from one life into another.

Bird in the House

A gift, you said, when we found it.
    And because my mother was dead,

I thought the cat had left it for me. The bird
    was black as omen, like a single crow

meaning sorrow. It was the year
    you'd remarried, summer —

the fields high and the pond reflecting
    everything: the willow, the small dock,

the crow overhead that — doubled —
    should have been an omen for joy.

Forgive me, Father, that I brought to that house
    my grief. You will not recall telling me

you could not understand my loss, not until
    your own mother died. Each night I'd wake

from a dream, my heart battering my rib cage —
    a trapped, wild bird. I did not know then

the cat had brought in a second grief: what was it
    but animal knowledge? Forgive me

that I searched for meaning in everything
      you did, that I watched you bury the bird

in the backyard — your back to me; I saw you
      flatten the mound, erasing it into the dirt.

Torna Atrás

AFTER *De Albina y Español, Nace Torna Atrás*
(From Albino and Spaniard, a Return-Backwards Is Born),
ANONYMOUS, C. 1785–1790

The unknown artist has rendered the father a painter and so
we see him at his work: painting a portrait of his wife—
their dark child watching nearby, a servant grinding colors
in the corner. The woman poses just beyond his canvas
and cannot see her likeness, her less than mirror image
coming to life beneath his hand. He has rendered her
homely, so unlike the woman we see in this scene, dressed
in late-century fashion, a *chicqueador*—mark of beauty
in the shape of a crescent moon—affixed to her temple.
If I say his painting is unfinished, that he has yet to make her
beautiful, to match the elegant sweep of her hair,
the graceful tilt of her head, has yet to adorn her dress
with lace and trim, it is only one way to see it. You might see,
instead, that the artist—perhaps to show his own skill—
has made the father a dilettante, incapable of capturing
his wife's beauty. Or, that he cannot see it: his mind's eye
reducing her to what he's made, as if to reveal the illusion
immanent in her flesh. If you consider the century's mythology
of the body—that a dark spot marked the genitals of anyone
with African blood—you might see how the black moon
on her white face recalls it: the *roseta* she passes to her child
marking him *torna atrás*. If I tell you such terms were born
in the Enlightenment's hallowed rooms, that the wages of empire
is myopia, you might see the father's vision as desire embodied

in paint, this rendering of his wife born of need to see himself
as architect of Truth, benevolent patriarch, father of uplift
ordering his domain. And you might see why, to understand
my father, I look again and again at this painting: how it is
that a man could love — and so diminish what he loves.

Enlightenment

In the portrait of Jefferson that hangs
    at Monticello, he is rendered two-toned:
his forehead white with illumination —

a lit bulb — the rest of his face in shadow,
    darkened as if the artist meant to contrast
his bright knowledge, its dark subtext.

By 1805, when Jefferson sat for the portrait,
    he was already linked to an affair
with his slave. Against a backdrop, blue

and ethereal, a wash of paint that seems
    to hold him in relief, Jefferson gazes out
across the centuries, his lips fixed as if

he's just uttered some final word.
    The first time I saw the painting, I listened
as my father explained the contradictions:

how Jefferson hated slavery, though — *out*
    of necessity, my father said — had to own
slaves; that his moral philosophy meant

he could not have fathered those children:
    would have been impossible, my father said.
For years we debated the distance between

word and deed. I'd follow my father from book
        to book, gathering citations, listen
as he named — like a field guide to Virginia —

each flower and tree and bird as if to prove
        a man's pursuit of knowledge is greater
than his shortcomings, the limits of his vision.

I did not know then the subtext
        of our story, that my father could imagine
Jefferson's words made flesh in my flesh —

the improvement of the blacks in body
        and mind, in the first instance of their mixture
with the whites — or that my father could believe

he'd made me *better.* When I think of this now,
        I see how the past holds us captive,
its beautiful ruin etched on the mind's eye:

my young father, a rough outline of the old man
        he's become, needing to show me
the better measure of his heart, an equation

writ large at Monticello. That was years ago.
        Now, we take in how much has changed:
talk of Sally Hemings, someone asking,

How white was she? — parsing the fractions
        as if to name what made her worthy
of Jefferson's attentions: a near-white,

quadroon mistress, not a plain black slave.
  Imagine stepping back into the past,
our guide tells us then — and I can't resist

whispering to my father: *This is where*
  we split up. I'll head around to the back.
When he laughs, I know he's grateful

I've made a joke of it, this history
  that links us — white father, black daughter —
even as it renders us other to each other.

Elegy

FOR MY FATHER

I think by now the river must be thick
    with salmon. Late August, I imagine it

as it was that morning: drizzle needling
    the surface, mist at the banks like a net

settling around us—everything damp
    and shining. That morning, awkward

and heavy in our hip waders, we stalked
    into the current and found our places—

you upstream a few yards and out
    far deeper. You must remember how

the river seeped in over your boots
    and you grew heavier with that defeat.

All day I kept turning to watch you, how
    first you mimed our guide's casting

then cast your invisible line, slicing the sky
    between us; and later, rod in hand, how

you tried—again and again—to find
    that perfect arc, flight of an insect

skimming the river's surface. Perhaps
    you recall I cast my line and reeled in

two small trout we could not keep.
    Because I had to release them, I confess,

I thought about the past—working
    the hooks loose, the fish writhing

in my hands, each one slipping away
    before I could let go. I can tell you now

that I tried to take it all in, record it
    for an elegy I'd write—one day—

when the time came. Your daughter,
    I was that ruthless. What does it matter

if I tell you I *learned* to be? You kept casting
    your line, and when it did not come back

empty, it was tangled with mine. Some nights,
    dreaming, I step again into the small boat

that carried us out and watch the bank receding—
    my back to where I know we are headed.

VI

ARTICULATION

Repentance

To make it right   Vermeer painted   then painted over
this scene   a woman alone at a table   the cloth pushed back
rough folds at the edge   as if   someone   had risen
in haste   abandoning the chair   beside her   a wineglass
nearly empty   just   in her reach   Though she's been called
idle and drunken   a woman drowsing   you might see
in her gesture   melancholia   Eyelids drawn
she rests   her head   in her hand   Beyond her   a still life
white jug   bowl of fruit   a goblet overturned   Before this
a man stood   in the doorway   a dog lay   on the floor
Perhaps   to exchange   loyalty   for betrayal
Vermeer erased   the dog   and made   of the man
a mirror   framed   by the open door   *Pentimento*
the word   for a painter's change   of heart   revision
on canvas   means the same   as remorse   after sin
Were she to rise   a mirror   behind her   the woman
might see   herself   as I did   turning   to rise
from my table   then back as if   into   Vermeer's scene
It was after   the quarrel   after   you'd had   again
too much   to drink   after   the bottle   did not shatter   though
I'd brought it   down hard   on the table   and the dog
had crept   from the room   to hide   Later   I found
a trace   of what I'd done   bruise on the table   the size
of my thumb   Worrying it   I must have looked   as she does

eyes downcast   my head   on the heel   of my palm   In paint
a story can change   mistakes be   undone   Imagine
Still Life   with Father   and Daughter   a moment so
far back   there's still time   to take the glass   from your hand
or mine

My Father as Cartographer

In dim light now, his eyes
    straining to survey
the territory: here is the country
    of *Loss,* its colony *Grief;*
the great continent *Desire*
    and its borderland *Regret;*

vast, unfathomable water,
    an archipelago — the tiny islands
of *Joy,* untethered, set adrift.
    At the bottom of the map
his legend and cartouche,
    the measures of distance, key

to the symbols marking each
    known land. What's missing
is the traveler's warning
    at the margins: a dragon —
its serpentine signature — monstrous
    as a two-faced daughter.

Duty

When he tells the story now
he's at the center of it,

everyone else in the house
falling into the backdrop—

my mother, grandmother,
an uncle, all dead now—props

in our story: father and daughter
caught in memory's half-light.

I'm too young to recall it,
so his story becomes *the* story:

1969, Hurricane Camille
bearing down, the old house

shuddering as if it will collapse.
Rain pours into every room

and he has to keep moving,
keep me out of harm's way—

a father's first duty: to protect.
And so, in the story, he does:

I am small in his arms, perhaps
even sleeping. Water is rising

around us and there is no
higher place he can take me

than this, memory forged
in the storm's eye: a girl

clinging to her father. What
can I do but this? Let him

tell it again and again as if
it's always been only us,

and that, when it mattered,
he was the one who saved me.

Reach

AFTER MY FATHER

Right off I hear him singing, the strings
of his old guitar hemming the darkness
as before—late nights on the front porch—
the mountains across the valley blurred
to outline. We are at it again, father
and daughter, deep in our cups, rehearsing
the long years between us. In the distance
I hear the foghorn call of bullfrogs,
envoys from the river of lamentation
my father is determined to cross. Already
I know where this is headed: how many times
has the night turned toward regret? My father
saying, *If only I'd been a better husband*
she'd be alive today, saying, *Gwen and I*
would get back together if she were alive.
It's the same old song. He is Orpheus
trying to bring her back with the music
of his words, lines of a poem drifting now
into my dream. Picking the first chords,
my father leans into the neck of the guitar,
rolls his shoulders until he's lost in it—
the song carrying him across the porch
and down into the damp grass. Even asleep,

I know where he is going. I cannot call
him back. Through the valley the blacktop
winds like a river, and he is stepping into it,
walking now toward the other side where
she waits, my mother, just out of reach.

Waterborne

AFTER ELLEN GALLAGHER'S *Watery Ecstatic*

Often I am permitted to return to a meadow
as if it were a given property of the mind . . .
      — Robert Duncan

As now, this meadow of seagrass, tangle
    of history — a nest of myriad,

mirrored faces. How not to think of words
    like *cargo* and *jettison,* each syllable

a last breath, vesicles rising to the surface
    of the sea. How not to think of loss,

how it takes hold and grows: like lacuna
    snails, slow and deliberate, on a reed?

Why is everything I see the past
    I've tried to forget? In dreams

I am a child again, underwater, my limbs
    sluggish as I struggle to wake. Always,

I am pursued. Waking, I am freighted
    with memory: my mother's last words

spoken—after her death—in a dream: *Do you know what it means*

to have a wound that never heals?
　　　　And now this thirst:

how many times have I cupped my hands
　　　　to drink, found—in the map

of my palms—this same pattern: lines
　　　　crossed and capillary as veins

in the body, these willowy reeds?
　　　　How can I see anything

but this: how trauma lives in the sea
　　　　of my body, awash in the waters

of forgetting. In every resilient blade
　　　　I see the ancestors, my mother's face.

Shooting Wild

At the theater I learn *shooting wild,*
a movie term that means filming a scene
without sound, and I think of being a child
watching my mother, how quiet she'd been,

soundless in our house made silent by fear.
At first her gestures were hard to understand,
and her hush when my stepfather was near.
Then one morning, the imprint of his hand

dark on her face, I learned to watch her more:
the way her grip tightened on a fork, night
after night; how a glance held me, the door—
a sign that made the need to hear so slight

I can't recall her voice since she's been dead:
no sound of her, no words she might have said.

Letter to Inmate #271847,
Convicted of Murder, 1985

When I heard you might get out, I was driving through the Delta, rain pounding my windshield, the sun angled and bright beneath dark clouds—familiar weather, what I'd learned long ago to call *the devil beating his wife*. I was listening to two things at once: an old song on the radio and, on the phone, a woman from Victim Services—her voice solicitous, slow, as though she were speaking to a child. I was back in the state I still call *home,* headed south on Highway 49, trying to resurrect my mother in the landscape of childhood as the Temptations were singing her song—the one she'd played over and over our last year in Mississippi, 1971, that summer before we moved to the city that would lead us, soon, to you. It was *Just My Imagination* and I could see her again: her back to me, swaying over the ironing board, the iron's steel plate catching the sun and holding it there. For a moment I was who I had been before, the joyful daughter of my young mother—until the woman on the phone said your name, telling me I must write the parole board a letter. I was again stepdaughter, daughter of sorrow, daughter of the murdered woman. This is how the past interrupts our lives, all of it entering the same doorway—like the hole in the trunk of my neighbor's tree: at once a natural shelter, haven for small creatures, but also evidence of injury, an entrance for decay. When I saw it, I thought of how, as a child, I'd have chosen it for play—a place to crawl inside and hide. And when I thought of hiding, I could not help but think of you. What does it mean to be safe in the world? Everywhere I go she is with me—my long-dead mother. Is there nowhere I might go and not find you, there too?

Meditation at Decatur Square

1

In which I try to decipher
           the story it tells,
this syntax of monuments
        flanking the old courthouse:
              here, a rough outline
like the torso of a woman
           great with child —
               a steatite boulder from which
        the Indians girdled the core
                    to make of it a bowl,
           and left in the stone a wound; here,

the bronze figure of Thomas Jefferson,
           quill in hand, inscribing
        a language of freedom,
                    a creation story —
           his hand poised at the word
happiness. There is not yet an ending,
           no period — the single mark,
intended or misprinted, that changes
        the meaning of everything.

Here too, for the Confederacy,
                an obelisk, oblivious
          in its name — a word
                that also meant the symbol
to denote, in ancient manuscripts,
          the *spurious, corrupt,* or *doubtful;*
                    at its base, forged
                in concrete, a narrative
of *valor, virtue, states' rights.*

Here, it is only the history of a word,
          obelisk,
          that points us toward
                what's not there; all of it
palimpsest, each mute object
          repeating a single refrain:

          Remember this.

2

Listen, there is another story I want
        this place to tell: I was a child here,

traveling to school through the heart of town
        by train, emerging into the light

of the square, in the shadow of the courthouse,
        a poetics of grief already being written.

This is the place to which I vowed
        I'd never return, hallowed ground now,

the new courthouse enshrining
        the story of my mother's death —

her autopsy, the police reports, even
        the smallest details: how first

her ex-husband's bullet entered
        her raised left hand, shattering the finger

on which she'd worn her rings; how tidy
        her apartment that morning, nothing

out of place but for, on the kitchen counter,
        a folding knife, a fifty-cent roll of coins.

3

Once, a poet wrote: *Books live in the mind*
like honey inside a beehive. When I read
those words to my brother, after his release,
this is what he said: *Inside the hive of prison*
my mind lived in books. Inside, everything
was a story unfinished: the letters he wrote
for inmates who could not write, who waited
each day for an answer to arrive; the library
with too few books, the last pages ripped out
so someone could roll a cigarette. To get by,
he read those books, conjuring new endings
where the stories stopped. Inside, everything
was possibility, each graving a pathway, one
word closer to the day he'd walk out of prison
into the rest of his story—a happy one or not,
depending on where you marked the ending.

4

I have counted the years   I am
a counter of years   ten   twenty

thirty now   So much gone and yet
she lives in my mind like a book

to which I keep returning   even
as the story remains the same

her ending   the space she left
a wound   a womb   a bowl hewn

Transfiguration

Today, it is not the shape of a bell, though I think of bells sounding

somewhere in the distance as we left you—each sound wave rippling

to the next: the shape of singing. Nor is it round, though round

is an echo: shape of the chamber, the bullet, the hole bored through skin.

It is not, now, the sign you drew across your body, your hands tracing—

again and again—a prayer: *Deliver me, Lord, from mine enemies.*

And though it haunts me, the shape of loss is not the chalked outline,

simulacrum on the pavement, on the report—an X each place

your life seeped out. Today, the fig tree in winter stopped me.

Limned in snow, the dark tree mimicked its shadow, twinned

branches curving inward, a nest of bones. For a moment I watched

the bright cardinal perch there, then beat its wings in flight.

Articulation

AFTER MIGUEL CABRERA'S PORTRAIT OF
SAINT GERTRUDE, 1763

In the legend, Saint Gertrude is called to write
after seeing, in a vision, the sacred heart of Christ.

Cabrera paints her among the instruments
of her faith: quill, inkwell, an open book,

rings on her fingers like Christ's many wounds—
the heart emblazoned on her chest, the holy

infant nestled there as if sunk deep in a wound.
Against the dark backdrop, her face is a wafer

of light. How not to see, in the saint's image,
my mother's last portrait: the dark backdrop,

her dress black as a habit, the bright edge
of her afro ringing her face with light? And how

not to recall her many wounds: ring finger
shattered, her ex-husband's bullet finding

her temple, lodging where her last thought lodged?
Three weeks gone, my mother came to me

in a dream, her body whole again but for
one perfect wound, the singular articulation

of all of them: a hole, center of her forehead,
the size of a wafer — light pouring from it.

How, then, could I not answer her life
with mine, she who saved me with hers?

And how could I not — bathed in the light
of her wound — find my calling there?

NOTES

Bellocq's Ophelia

Ophelia is the imagined name of a prostitute photographed around 1912 by E. J. Bellocq, later collected in the book *Storyville Portraits*. A white-skinned black woman—mulatto, quadroon, or octoroon—she would have lived in one of the few "colored" brothels, such as Willie Piazza's Basin Street Mansion or Lula White's Mahogany Hall, which, according to the Blue Book, was known as the Octoroon Club.

Native Guard

Epigraph (page 53)
From "Meditation on Form and Measure," in *Black Zodiac* by Charles Wright (Farrar, Straus and Giroux, 1997).

"Genus Narcissus"
Epigraph from "To Daffadills" by Robert Herrick (1591–1674).

Epigraph (page 71)
From "Mississippi Goddamn," on *In Concert* by Nina Simone. Verve Records, 1964.

"Pilgrimage"
The question *What is to become / of all the living things in this place?* is from *My Cave Life in Vicksburg* by Mary Webster Loughborough (New York, 1864).

"Native Guard"
Epigraph from the "Address at the Grave of the Unknown Dead" by Frederick Douglass, Arlington, Virginia, May 30, 1871; quoted in *Race and Reunion: The Civil War in American Memory* by David Blight (Belknap Press, 2001).

The first regiments of the Louisiana Native Guards were mustered into service in September, October, and November of 1862—the 1st Regiment thus becoming the first officially sanctioned regiment of black soldiers in the Union Army, and the 2nd and 3rd made up of men who had been slaves only months before enlisting. During the war, the fort at Ship Island, Mississippi, called Fort Massachusetts, was maintained as a prison for Confederate soldiers—military convicts and prisoners of war—manned by the 2nd Regiment. Among the 2nd Regiment's officers was Francis E. Dumas—the son of a white Creole father and a mulatto mother—who had inherited slaves when his father died. Although Louisiana law had prohibited him from manumitting these slaves, when he joined the Union Army, Dumas freed them and encouraged those men of age to join the Native Guards. From *The Louisiana Native Guards: The Black Military Experience During the Civil War* by James G. Hollandsworth (Louisiana State University Press, 1995).

"Native Guard," *January 1863*
The Union ship *Northern Star* transported seven companies of the 2nd Louisiana Native Guards to Fort Massachusetts, Ship Island, on January 12, 1863. The lines ". . . I can look out / upon the Gulf and see the surf breaking, / tossing the ships, the great gunboats bobbing / on the water. And are we not the same, / slaves in the hands of the master, destiny?" are borrowed, in slightly different form, from *Thank God My Regiment an African One: The Civil War Diary of Colonel Nathan W. Daniels,* edited by C. P. Weaver (Louisiana State University Press, 1998).

"Native Guard," *April 1863*
On April 9, 1863, 180 black men and their officers went onto the mainland to meet Confederate troops near Pascagoula, Mississippi. After the skirmish, as the black troops were retreating (having been outnumbered by the Confederates), white Union troops on board the gunboat *Jackson* fired directly at them and not at oncoming Confederates. Several black soldiers were killed or wounded. The phrases *an unfortunate incident* and *their names shall deck the page of history* are also from *Thank God My Regiment an African One: The Civil War Diary of Colonel Nathan W. Daniels.*

"Native Guard," *May 1863*
During the Battle of Port Hudson in May 1863, General Nathaniel P. Banks requested a truce to locate the wounded Union soldiers and bury the dead. His troops, however, ignored the area where the Native Guards had fought, leaving those men unclaimed. When Colonel W. B. Shelby, a Confederate officer, asked permission to bury those putrefying bodies in front of his lines, Banks refused, saying that he had

no dead in that area. From *The Louisiana Native Guards: The Black Military Experience During the Civil War.*

"Native Guard," *1865*
In April 1864, Confederate troops attacked Fort Pillow, a Union garrison fifty miles north of Memphis. One correspondent, in a dispatch to the *Mobile Advertiser and Register,* reported that, after gaining control of the fort, the Confederates disregarded several individual attempts by the black troops to surrender, and "an indiscriminate slaughter followed" in which Colonel Nathan Bedford Forrest purportedly ordered the black troops "shot down like dogs." From "The Fort Pillow Massacre: Assessing the Evidence" by John Cimprich, in *Black Soldiers in Blue: African-American Troops in the Civil War Era,* edited by John David Smith (University of North Carolina Press, 2002).

"Again, the Fields"
After Winslow Homer's *The Veteran in a New Field,* 1865.
Epigraph quoted in Bell Irvin Wiley and Horst D. Milhollen, *They Who Fought Here* (Macmillan, 1959).

"Pastoral"
The final line — "*You don't hate the South?* they ask. *You don't hate it?*" — is borrowed, in slightly different form, from William Faulkner's character Quentin Compson at the end of *Absalom, Absalom!:* "I don't hate the south. I don't hate it."

"Elegy for the Native Guards"
Epigraph from "Ode to the Confederate Dead" by Allen Tate, 1937.

"South"
Epigraph from *Consilience: The Unity of Knowledge* by E. O. Wilson (Knopf, 1998).

Thrall

"Miracle of the Black Leg"
The texts and images referred to in "Miracle of the Black Leg" are discussed in *The Phantom Limb Phenomenon: A Medical, Folkloric, and Historical Study — Texts and*

Translations of Tenth- to Twentieth-Century Accounts of the Miraculous Restoration of Lost Body Parts by Douglas B. Price, M.D., and Neil J. Twombly, S.J., Ph.D. (Georgetown University Press, 1978), and in *One Leg in the Grave: The Miracle of the Transplantation of the Black Leg by the Saints Cosmas and Damian* by Kees W. Zimmerman (Elsevier/Bunge, 1998). Representations of the myth appear in Greek narratives, in a Scottish poem, and in paintings and altarpieces in Spain, Italy, Germany, Austria, Portugal, Switzerland, France, and Belgium.

"Taxonomy"
Casta paintings illustrated the various mixed unions in colonial Mexico and the children of those unions, whose names and taxonomies were recorded in the *Book of Castas.* The widespread belief in the "taint" of black blood — that it was irreversible —resulted in taxonomies rooted in language that implied a "return backwards." From *Casta Painting: Images of Race in Eighteenth-Century Mexico* by Ilona Katzew (Yale University Press, 2004).

"Thrall"
Juan de Pareja (1606–1670) was the slave of the artist Diego Velázquez until his manumission in 1650. For many years Pareja served Velázquez as a laborer in his studio and later sat for the portrait *Juan de Pareja,* which Velázquez painted in order to practice for creating a portrait of Pope Innocent X. Pareja was also a painter, and is best known for his work *The Calling of Saint Matthew.* From *El Museo pictórico y escala óptica,* volume 3, by Antonio Palomino (Madrid, 1947, p. 913; originally published in 1724).

ACKNOWLEDGMENTS

Thanks to the editors of the following journals, in which these poems, sometimes in different versions, first appeared.

Academy of American Poets, Poem-a-Day, poets.org: "Imperatives for Carrying On in the Aftermath." *The Atlantic:* "Articulation." *The Georgia Review:* "Letter to Inmate #271847, Convicted of Murder, 1985" and "Meditation at Decatur Square." *Margie / American Journal of Poetry:* "Transfiguration." *The National:* "Reach." *The New Yorker:* "Repentance." *Poet Lore:* "My Father as Cartographer" and "Shooting Wild." *Poetry London:* "Waterborne." *Time:* "Duty."

"Imperatives for Carrying On in the Aftermath" was reprinted in *The Pushcart Prize Anthology: Best of the Small Presses 2017.* "Shooting Wild" was reprinted in *The Best American Poetry 2018.*